10 to 25:

The Science of Motivating

Young People

Amanda J. Sterling

Content

Introduction

If you've ever looked at a teenager slouched on the couch, scrolling endlessly through their phone, and thought, *"Why don't they care?"* — you're not alone. Parents, teachers, and mentors across the world are asking the same question. How can someone so bright, curious, and capable seem so uninterested, distracted, or unmotivated?

The answer isn't laziness. It's neuroscience.

Between the ages of 10 and 25, the human brain undergoes a transformation as dramatic as early childhood. During these fifteen years, the brain rewires itself for independence, identity, and purpose. It learns not just *what* to think, but *why* to act. Motivation — that inner drive that pushes us toward growth — is built from the inside out. And it develops differently than most adults realize.

Understanding this process changes everything.

The Myth of the "Lazy Generation"

Every generation of adults has looked at the one that follows and shaken its head. In the 1950s, it was "rebellious teenagers." In the 1990s, "apathetic slackers." Today, we hear about "screen-obsessed Gen Z." But when you look past the headlines, young people today are *not* less motivated — they're motivated by different things.

They crave autonomy (the freedom to make meaningful choices), connection (belonging and validation), and purpose (a sense that what they do matters). When those needs are met, their motivation can be unstoppable. But when those same needs are ignored — when they're pressured, judged, or misunderstood — motivation doesn't vanish. It simply turns inward or sideways.

A student might not care about algebra homework, but they'll spend ten focused hours building a Minecraft world. A young adult may resist career advice from a parent but obsess over learning music production or coding. The drive is there. What's missing is alignment.

Motivation hasn't disappeared. It's just gone underground.

The Adolescent Brain: A Work in Progress

To understand why motivation looks so unpredictable between ages 10 and 25, we need to peek under the hood of the developing brain.

During adolescence, the prefrontal cortex — the part of the brain responsible for planning, focus, and self-control — is still under construction. Meanwhile, the limbic system, which governs emotion, reward, and social connection, is firing at full intensity. In other words: feelings are at their peak before regulation catches up.

This developmental gap explains a lot. Teenagers and young adults experience the world in high definition — emotions feel stronger, risks seem worth taking, and boredom feels unbearable. Dopamine, the brain's motivation chemical, is constantly whispering, *"What's next? What's exciting? What's meaningful?"*

That's not dysfunction — it's design. The adolescent brain is wired to explore, test limits, and learn through experience. It's practicing how to become independent. And when adults misread that process as defiance or apathy, we risk breaking the very motivation we're trying to build.

Motivation Is a Conversation, Not a Command

Many of the strategies we use to "motivate" young people actually do the opposite. Rewards, punishments, and constant reminders can create temporary compliance, but rarely lasting drive. That's because motivation doesn't grow in an environment of control — it grows in an environment of trust and collaboration.

When a parent says, "Do it because I said so," they're triggering resistance, not responsibility. When a teacher says, "You need to care more," the student often hears, *"You're not enough."*

What works better? Curiosity. Connection. Autonomy. Instead of *telling* a young person what to value, we ask *what matters to them* — and then connect that to learning, growth, or effort.

For example:

⇒ "What's something you've worked hard at recently?"

⇒ "How did it feel when you got better at it?"

⇒ "What do you wish adults understood about what motivates you?"

These questions open doors. They turn motivation into a shared discovery, not a power struggle.

The "Invisible Work" of Growing Up

Between 10 and 25, young people are doing more than studying or socializing. They're building an identity — a sense of self that can stand on its own. This is invisible work, and it takes enormous energy.

Imagine if you woke up one day in a body that felt unfamiliar, in a world full of expectations, with your future depending on choices you barely understand. That's adolescence. Every decision — what to wear, who to befriend, what to believe — feels like a test. It's no wonder motivation sometimes looks inconsistent.

But that inconsistency isn't failure. It's feedback. It shows where a young person's identity, values, and confidence are still forming. When adults interpret that as laziness, they miss an opportunity to guide the process with compassion instead of control.

Our job isn't to *force* motivation. It's to *understand* it.

The Science of Support

Research in developmental psychology and neuroscience shows that young people thrive when three key needs are met:

1. Autonomy – "I have a voice."

2. Competence – "I can do this."

3. Relatedness – "I belong."

These are not luxuries. They are the building blocks of intrinsic motivation. When a teen or young adult feels controlled, incompetent, or isolated, motivation withers. But when they feel empowered, capable, and connected, drive comes naturally.

This explains why coaching, mentoring, and parenting approaches rooted in *supportive guidance* are far more effective than those built on *pressure or punishment*. The goal isn't to make young people obey — it's to help them believe in their own ability to act with purpose.

A Generation Searching for Meaning

Today's youth are growing up in a world of contradictions: limitless information but scarce direction, constant connection but deep loneliness, more opportunity than ever but less clarity about identity and purpose.

They're not unmotivated — they're overwhelmed. They need meaning to focus their energy. That's why so many young people light up when they find a cause, a passion, or a project that feels personal. They want their effort to matter. When adults can connect that desire to real-world goals, we ignite something powerful: purpose-driven motivation.

This is where science meets empathy. Motivation isn't just about brain chemistry or parenting techniques — it's about helping young people answer a simple but profound question:

"Why should I try?"

When they can answer that in their own voice, motivation becomes self-sustaining.

What This Book Will Teach You

10 to 25 is not another rulebook on how to "fix" young people. It's a guide to understanding how motivation develops — biologically, emotionally, and socially — and how adults can nurture it through practical, research-backed strategies.

You'll learn:

⇒ How brain development influences motivation, emotion, and decision-making.

⇒ Why some forms of praise and feedback kill drive while others build it.

⇒ How to help teens and young adults develop grit, self-regulation, and resilience.

⇒ How to create environments — at home, school, or work — that inspire curiosity instead of compliance.

⇒ How to connect motivation to values and purpose in an age of distraction.

Each chapter blends neuroscience, psychology, and real-life stories from classrooms, families, and youth programs around the world. You'll find exercises, conversation prompts, and reflection questions that help turn insights into action.

This isn't about making young people do more. It's about helping them *want* to do more — by understanding the science of what truly drives them.

A New Way Forward

If you've ever felt frustrated, confused, or helpless trying to motivate a young person, you're in the right place. The frustration you feel is real — but it's not because they don't care.

It's because their brain and identity are under construction, and they're learning how to steer.

Your role isn't to take the wheel. It's to sit beside them, help them read the map, and remind them that the journey is theirs to make.

Motivation isn't something we give to young people. It's something we build with them. And when we do, the results can be extraordinary.

Part I

The Adolescent Brain and the Roots of Motivation

Chapter 1 — The Brain Under Construction

Why the Teenage Brain Isn't Broken — It's Becoming Extraordinary

Sixteen-year-old Maya lies on her bed, phone in hand, a math worksheet untouched beside her. Her mother leans against the doorframe.

"You've been scrolling for an hour. Don't you care about your grades?"
Maya sighs. "I'll do it later, Mom."

To an adult, it looks like apathy. But inside Maya's head, one of the most powerful neurological transformations of her life is underway. Between the ages of 10 and 25, the brain is in full renovation mode — rewiring connections, reshaping priorities, and redefining motivation from the inside out.

A Brain Mid-Renovation

Adolescence is like living in a house that's being remodeled while you still occupy it. Everything functions, but nothing feels finished.

The brain begins trimming away neural connections that are no longer useful — a process called synaptic pruning — while strengthening the ones that are used most often. It's efficiency through subtraction. What remains becomes faster, sharper, and more specialized.

This remodeling explains why teenagers can learn new skills at lightning speed but struggle with consistency. Their brains are literally reorganizing how attention, planning, and reward interact. It's not a lack of motivation — it's an excess of neural construction dust.

The Balance Problem

One of the great paradoxes of adolescence is that the emotional brain matures faster than the logical brain. The limbic system, which drives emotion and reward, comes online early, while the prefrontal cortex, responsible for self-control and long-term planning, won't fully mature until the mid-twenties.

In other words, the accelerator is installed before the brakes.

That's why teens often act before thinking, or seem passionately driven one moment and indifferent the next. They're learning how to coordinate emotion, impulse, and logic

— a process that takes years of practice, feedback, and patience from adults.

Motivation Runs on Meaning

Because their prefrontal cortex is still developing, young people are guided less by reason ("I should do this") and more by emotion and relevance ("This matters to me"). They aren't unmotivated — they're selectively motivated. They care deeply about things that feel authentic, social, or meaningful, and quickly disengage from things that feel forced or pointless.

That's why a teen who seems lazy about school might pour hours into music production or gaming. In both cases, the same dopamine system — the brain's reward network — is active. It just responds more strongly to novelty and connection than obligation.

When we link effort to meaning ("This skill helps you express yourself" instead of "Do this for a grade"), motivation rises naturally.

Risk and Reward

Adults often see risk-taking as reckless, but for the developing brain, risk is rehearsal. Exploring boundaries, testing independence, and chasing new experiences are ways the brain learns confidence and judgment. Without risk, growth stalls.

Our job isn't to remove risk but to redirect it. Encourage challenges that stretch, not endanger — from creative projects to sports, volunteering, or travel. Each healthy risk activates the same reward pathways as rebellion, but with far better outcomes.

The Power of Social Motivation

Few forces shape teenage motivation like belonging. During adolescence, the brain becomes hypersensitive to social approval and rejection. MRI studies show that being accepted by peers activates the same reward centers as winning money.

That's why friendships, online communities, and group identity matter so deeply. They provide a sense of safety and significance that fuels effort and perseverance. When adults dismiss social priorities as "drama," they miss an enormous motivational engine.

When guided wisely — through teamwork, service, or shared goals — social belonging can transform distraction into purpose.

Emotion as Energy

Teen emotions are intense, unpredictable, and often exhausting — for both them and us. But emotion isn't the enemy of reason; it's the spark of motivation. Feelings tell the brain what's important enough to remember and act on. When we teach young people to recognize and regulate emotions instead of suppressing them, we give them the tools to use that energy productively.

Helping them move from "I'm so angry" to "I'm frustrated because this matters to me" builds the emotional intelligence that supports motivation for life.

The Adult's Role

Supporting a brain under construction requires scaffolding, not control. We can't rush development, but we can create environments where motivation grows naturally:

1. Provide choice. Let them own small decisions — it builds autonomy.

2. Encourage effort, not outcomes. "I see how hard you're working" rewires motivation more effectively than "You're so smart."

3.　　Connect tasks to identity. Frame challenges as part of who they're becoming, not just what they're doing.

4.　　Model calm curiosity. When you stay patient, you teach emotional regulation by example.

Every supportive response literally shapes brain wiring toward resilience and self-motivation.

Becoming Extraordinary

By the time the brain finishes developing around age 25, emotional intensity and cognitive control are finally in sync. The very traits that made adolescence messy — risk-taking, passion, idealism — become the foundation of creativity, leadership, and purpose.

The teenage brain isn't broken; it's becoming extraordinary. It's learning how to transform feeling into focus, and impulse into intention. Our task is not to fix it, but to understand and guide it—patiently, wisely, and with faith in what it's becoming.

The Takeaway

Adolescence is not a problem to solve — it's a process to support. The teenage brain isn't failing; it's *forging*. Every moment of inconsistency, emotion, or resistance is part of the wiring process that will one day make motivation self-sustaining.

When we understand that young people's apparent chaos is actually construction, everything changes. We stop reacting with frustration and start responding with faith. Their distraction isn't defiance — it's development. Their risk-taking isn't recklessness — it's rehearsal for independence.

Motivation during these years will never look tidy or predictable, because it's being built from the ground up. But when adults provide trust, choice, and emotional safety, the brain learns that effort is rewarding and identity is self-directed.

So instead of asking, "How do I make them care?" we might ask, "How can I connect what matters to them with what will help them grow?" Instead of pushing harder, we can guide smarter — linking learning to meaning, autonomy to structure, and emotion to purpose.

The teenage brain is a masterpiece in progress. Beneath the impulsivity and uncertainty lies an engine of potential more powerful than at any other stage of life. With patience, empathy, and understanding, we don't just survive adolescence — we help it become what it was designed to be: the extraordinary laboratory of human motivation.

Chapter 2 — Wired for Reward, Not Routine

How Dopamine Shapes Curiosity, Drive, and Distraction

Fifteen-year-old Leo sits at his desk, a history assignment open in one window and a gaming stream in another. The cursor blinks patiently on his essay document. Ten minutes pass, then twenty. He knows he should start writing—but his brain is already chasing the flicker of excitement from the live chat.

This isn't a lack of discipline. It's neuroscience. Leo's brain, like every adolescent's, is tuned for reward, not routine. His internal chemistry is hunting for stimulation, novelty, and meaning—and the modern world offers it in unlimited supply.

To understand how to motivate a young person, we have to understand their brain's favorite molecule: dopamine.

The Dopamine System: Fuel for Motivation

Dopamine is often called the "pleasure chemical," but that's not quite right. It doesn't create pleasure itself—it drives us toward it. It's the neurotransmitter of anticipation, the chemical whisper that says, "Something exciting could happen if you just keep going."

For young people, dopamine plays a huge role in shaping motivation, attention, and risk-taking. The adolescent brain releases more dopamine in response to new experiences than the adult brain does. This makes teens and young adults naturally curious, experimental, and emotionally intense.

The flip side? Routine, repetition, and delayed gratification feel almost painful. What feels steady to adults can feel suffocating to someone whose brain is wired to chase reward and novelty.

The Search for "The Next Thing"

Between ages 10 and 25, the dopamine system is hypersensitive to what's next. It pushes the young person to explore, learn, and test boundaries. This biological drive once helped humans leave the safety of childhood and venture into the unknown.

Today, however, that same system is constantly hijacked by apps, games, and algorithms engineered to trigger dopamine bursts. Each notification, like, or level-up gives a small hit—just enough to keep the brain hooked in anticipation of the next one.

When dopamine becomes linked primarily to digital rewards, real-world motivation can start to fade. Homework feels dull compared to the instant feedback of a glowing screen. Long-term goals lose their shine when short-term pleasure is one tap away.

This isn't moral weakness—it's chemistry out of balance.

The Routine Problem

Adolescents are often accused of being inconsistent. One day, they'll spend six hours mastering a song on guitar; the next, they can't stick with a 30-minute assignment. The difference lies in reward prediction.

When an activity feels personally meaningful, social, or novel, dopamine flows freely. But when the reward is delayed or imposed ("You have to do this"), motivation plummets. This is why external pressure—grades, nagging, or punishment— rarely sustains effort. It activates compliance, not curiosity.

Routine tasks still matter, of course—but they need context. When young people understand why something matters and how it connects to their goals or identity, dopamine reengages. The brain shifts from "I have to" to "I want to."

Harnessing the Dopamine Drive

If dopamine makes young people chase stimulation, the key isn't to eliminate it—it's to channel it. Adults can do this by creating environments that blend structure with novelty.

1.	Break big goals into small wins. Every milestone releases a mini burst of dopamine, reinforcing progress.

2.	Add novelty to repetition. Change study locations, rotate activities, or introduce creative twists. The brain craves freshness.

3.	Tie effort to emotion. Connect a task to something personally meaningful: "This project could help others," or "This skill gives you independence."

4.	Give autonomy. When young people feel ownership over their goals, dopamine activity increases. A sense of choice converts pressure into motivation.

5.	Use anticipation, not reward. Instead of saying, "If you finish, you'll get X," say, "Wait till you see what happens when you nail this." The brain loves curiosity.

By aligning motivation with the brain's natural reward system, we transform dopamine from a distraction trigger into a focus amplifier.

When Dopamine Turns Against Us

A chronically overstimulated dopamine system can lead to "reward fatigue." In this state, everyday pleasures—reading, learning, or simple conversation—feel dull compared to high-intensity digital or emotional experiences.

Young people begin chasing bigger hits: faster gratification, louder validation, more scrolling. This is why some teens describe feeling "bored all the time" even with endless entertainment. The brain isn't under-stimulated; it's overexposed.

The solution isn't withdrawal—it's a reset. Encouraging breaks from constant dopamine spikes (digital detoxes, outdoor activity, creative hobbies) helps recalibrate the reward system. After a few days, smaller, real-world joys begin to feel rewarding again.

Building Long-Term Motivation

One of the biggest milestones between 10 and 25 is learning to link short-term effort to long-term satisfaction. The adolescent brain is capable of extraordinary persistence—but only when it can see a future reward that feels emotionally real.

That's where adults come in. Our role isn't to supply motivation, but to connect dots:

⇒ "This isn't just homework; it's training your ability to focus."

⇒ "This skill could open doors to the life you want."

When effort becomes part of a personal story, dopamine stays engaged across time. What was once routine becomes meaningful.

The Takeaway

The young brain is not lazy—it's wired for reward. It craves stimulation, novelty, and connection because those are the pathways that teach independence and purpose. The challenge isn't to fight dopamine, but to guide it toward growth.

By designing learning, parenting, and mentoring experiences that engage curiosity instead of compliance, we align with biology rather than against it. And when that happens, motivation stops being a battle—and becomes a natural, unstoppable force.

Chapter 3 — The Psychology of Motivation

Why Autonomy, Mastery, and Purpose Matter Most

A teacher once told me about a student named Noah, a bright fifteen-year-old who rarely turned in homework. "He just doesn't care," she said. "But then one week, we started a group project on climate change — and suddenly he was leading the team. He researched late into the night, made slides, even argued with the principal for better recycling bins. Same kid. Totally different motivation."

What changed wasn't Noah's personality or intelligence. It was his psychological fuel. The project gave him *autonomy* (he chose the topic), *mastery* (he could see himself improving), and *purpose* (it mattered to something bigger than a grade). When those three needs align, motivation switches on like a light.

These are the universal ingredients of drive — for kids, teens, and adults alike. They're not tricks or rewards, but deep human needs rooted in how our brains evolved to learn and grow.

Autonomy: The Power of Choice

From childhood, humans crave agency — the feeling of "I'm in control of what happens to me." Autonomy doesn't mean total freedom; it means having a voice. When young people feel forced, they resist. When they feel heard, they engage.

Psychologists Edward Deci and Richard Ryan, founders of Self-Determination Theory, found that autonomy is one of the three essential nutrients of intrinsic motivation. When someone chooses a goal because it feels personally meaningful, their effort is stronger, deeper, and more enduring.

Yet many well-intentioned adults unintentionally crush autonomy with constant oversight:

⇒ "Do it this way."

⇒ "Don't waste time."

⇒ "Because I said so."

The message heard by the adolescent brain? "You don't trust me."

Instead of dictating, we can guide.

⇒ "Which part of this do you want to start with?"

⇒ "How would you approach it?"

⇒ "What do you think would make it better?"

When adults offer structure *with* choice, motivation shifts from resistance to ownership. The same student who avoids chores might proudly tackle them if given control over the process: "Would you rather handle dishes or laundry tonight?"

Small freedoms signal big respect — and respect fuels responsibility.

Mastery: The Joy of Getting Better

The second pillar of motivation is mastery — the deep satisfaction of progress. Young people are born to learn, but somewhere along the way, learning starts to feel like judgment instead of discovery. Grades replace curiosity. Comparison replaces growth.

The developing brain craves challenge, but only if success feels *possible*. Too easy, and it's boring. Too hard, and it's discouraging. The sweet spot — what psychologist Lev Vygotsky called the "zone of proximal development" — is where growth feels exciting.

When adults praise only outcomes ("You got an A!"), motivation becomes fragile. The next failure feels like identity collapse. But when we praise effort and process ("You stuck with that problem even when it was hard"), the brain learns to associate persistence with reward. Dopamine fires, confidence rises, and progress becomes self-reinforcing.

Neuroscience shows that every time a young person overcomes a small challenge, their brain releases a subtle burst of dopamine — a signal that says, *keep going, this works*. That's how mastery builds resilience: not through perfection, but through the repeated pairing of effort and reward.

To cultivate mastery:

⇒ Frame mistakes as feedback, not failure.

⇒ Break big goals into small, visible steps.

⇒ Celebrate improvement, not just achievement.

When a teenager says, "I'm not good at this," they're not seeking praise — they're seeking hope that growth is still possible.

Purpose: The Deep Why

The third pillar — and often the most powerful — is purpose. Purpose gives effort meaning beyond immediate gratification. It answers the question, *Why should I care?*

Teens and young adults live in a world overflowing with choices but short on direction. When everything seems possible, it's easy to feel aimless. Purpose grounds motivation in identity: "This is who I want to be."

Purpose doesn't have to be world-changing. It can be as simple as "I want to help others," "I want to be independent," or "I want to make something beautiful." The moment effort connects to values, motivation transforms from *push* to *pull*.

Adults can help by asking open-ended questions:

⇒ "What kind of person do you want to be in five years?"

⇒ "What makes you proud when you work hard?"

⇒ "What would make this project matter to you?"

Even if they shrug or joke at first, these questions plant seeds. The brain starts looking for meaning — and finds it in unexpected places.

When young people feel that what they do matters, they stop working *for* rewards and start working *from* purpose.

The Motivation Formula

When autonomy, mastery, and purpose intersect, motivation becomes self-sustaining. Each element reinforces the others:

⇒   Autonomy gives ownership.

⇒   Mastery builds confidence.

⇒   Purpose provides direction.

Take away any one of them, and drive weakens. Too much control kills autonomy. Too much pressure kills mastery. Too little meaning kills purpose.

But when all three align, something extraordinary happens: effort feels natural. Young people push themselves not because they must, but because they *want* to see what they're capable of.

The Takeaway

Motivation isn't something we inject into the next generation. It's something we uncover by meeting their basic psychological needs.

Give them choice, and they'll show you initiative. Give them challenge, and they'll show you growth. Give them meaning, and they'll show you purpose.

The teenage brain is ready to work hard — but only for something that feels real, chosen, and worth doing. Our job is to help them find it.

Chapter 4 — From "Have To" to "Want To"

Turning External Pressure into Inner Drive

Every parent, teacher, or coach has said it: "You have to." You have to finish your homework. You have to clean your room. You have to show up on time. These demands come from love, responsibility, and a genuine wish to prepare young people for life. But to the developing brain, "have to" sounds like pressure, not purpose. It triggers resistance, not motivation.

The adolescent brain is built to seek autonomy — to test boundaries and decide who it wants to be. When every direction comes from outside, that natural drive for independence pushes back. The result is a power struggle that adults interpret as defiance but is really a sign of growth. The good news is that external expectations can become internal motivation if we know how to guide the shift.

Why Pressure Backfires

External pressure works in the short term but collapses in the long run. Rewards and punishments activate what psychologists call *extrinsic motivation*—the kind that depends on outside control. A teen might study to earn praise or avoid punishment, but once the reward disappears, so does the effort. Research shows that heavy reliance on external motivators often reduces creativity, curiosity, and resilience.

This doesn't mean young people should never face expectations. Structure and accountability matter. But when pressure is constant, the brain learns to associate work with anxiety rather than satisfaction. Tasks become obligations instead of opportunities.

Neuroscience confirms this. When people feel controlled, activity in the brain's reward circuits decreases. But when they feel a sense of choice and ownership, dopamine — the motivation messenger — increases. The difference between "I must" and "I want to" is chemical, not just emotional.

The Autonomy Shift

The key to transforming "have to" into "want to" is autonomy support — guiding without micromanaging. It's the difference between being a boss and being a coach.

Instead of saying, "You have to start your essay tonight," try, "What's your plan for getting it done this week?" Instead of, "Stop wasting time," ask, "What's making it hard to focus right now?"

These questions hand responsibility back to the young person. They invite reflection instead of rebellion. Even small choices — where to study, which topic to tackle first, or how to organize work — signal trust. And trust feeds motivation.

Autonomy doesn't mean absence of rules. It means creating space for ownership within clear boundaries. "You're responsible for your work, and I'm here to help if you get stuck" is far more effective than "Do it or else." The brain responds better to guidance than to control.

Internalizing Values

At some point, every adolescent faces the question: "Why should I care?" This is where adults often panic. But the question isn't disrespect — it's identity work. They're trying to connect actions to values.

Motivation becomes internalized when behavior aligns with something personally meaningful. A student who dislikes math might stay motivated if they understand it as part of their dream to design video games or build a business. A teen who resists chores might engage more if they see them as acts of contribution rather than compliance.

Adults can help bridge that gap with connection, not correction. Instead of giving a list of reasons, share a story:

"When I was your age, I didn't like doing this either. But I realized it made me more confident later." Personal examples turn abstract lessons into human ones. The goal isn't persuasion — it's empathy that invites reflection.

Motivation Through Language

The words we use can either fuel or drain motivation.

⇒ "You should" implies obligation.

⇒ "You could" implies opportunity.

⇒ "You get to" implies privilege.

Small shifts in language change how the brain interprets a task. "You have to practice piano" sounds like pressure. "You get to work on your favorite song" activates curiosity. The meaning changes, even if the task stays the same.

Similarly, emphasizing growth over performance transforms fear into focus. "Let's see how much progress you can make tonight" feels different from "Don't mess up again." Young people learn to associate effort with possibility rather than threat.

Building Inner Drive

Intrinsic motivation — the desire to act for its own sake — grows from three experiences: competence, connection, and choice. Every time adults nurture these, external pressure becomes less necessary.

1.   Competence: Create achievable challenges that show progress. Small wins keep dopamine flowing.

2.   Connection: Build relationships where feedback feels supportive, not judgmental.

3.   Choice: Give freedom within structure so responsibility feels earned, not imposed.

When those needs are met, effort feels self-directed. A teen might still grumble about chores or school, but underneath, they begin to feel pride in ownership. The "have to" starts transforming into "I did it."

The Takeaway

External motivation can start the engine, but only internal motivation keeps it running. Young people thrive when they understand the *why* behind expectations and feel trusted to steer their own effort. Adults don't need to remove structure — just redesign it around collaboration, not control.

The next time you're tempted to say, "You have to," pause and reframe it. "You can," "You're capable of," or "You get to" speaks to the part of the brain that hungers for growth, not obedience. When we trade pressure for partnership, we don't lose authority — we gain influence. And influence is what turns rules into self-motivation.

Chapter 5 — The Power of Identity

How Teens Build Their "Why"

Ask a teenager what they want to do with their life, and you'll often get a shrug, a nervous laugh, or a sarcastic reply like, "How am I supposed to know?" It's easy to mistake that uncertainty for indifference. In truth, adolescence is a time when one of the brain's biggest jobs is underway — constructing an identity. The "who am I?" question isn't a philosophical luxury; it's a developmental task. And the way young people answer it shapes everything about their motivation.

Identity gives effort direction. Without it, even the most talented or intelligent person struggles to care. With it, energy becomes purpose. Every choice, every risk, every setback begins to mean something. To help young people find motivation, we first have to help them find *themselves*.

The Adolescent Identity Project

During adolescence, the brain undergoes massive changes in how it processes social feedback and self-awareness. MRI studies show that regions involved in self-reflection become more active, while networks that track how others see us grow stronger. That's why teenagers seem hypersensitive to reputation, comparison, and belonging. They're not being dramatic — they're doing the work of identity construction.

Identity doesn't appear overnight. It's built like a collage: a mix of family values, peer influences, passions, and experiences. Each new experience asks the same silent question: "Is this me?" When a teenager experiments with music, fashion, activism, or new friendships, they're not rebelling — they're testing pieces of self. Adults often misread that exploration as instability, but it's actually the path to authenticity.

Psychologist Erik Erikson called this stage *identity versus role confusion*. It's the brain's way of sorting through possible selves — deciding what fits and what doesn't. The process is messy, but it's necessary. Without exploration, young people may adopt an identity by default rather than by choice, leaving them less motivated and more anxious later on.

Why Identity Fuels Motivation

Motivation thrives when behavior aligns with identity. People act most powerfully when they see their effort as an expression of who they are. "I'm studying because I'm curious" is stronger than "I'm studying because my teacher said so." "I'm training because I'm an athlete" sustains more effort than "I have to run today." When a young person's goals connect to their sense of self, effort feels natural.

This is why generic advice like "work harder" or "do better" rarely works. Motivation isn't a switch; it's a reflection. Teens are constantly asking, consciously or not, "What kind of person am I becoming?" If adults can connect action to that question — to values, to future selves, to personal meaning — drive follows.

One powerful technique is identity-based feedback. Instead of saying, "You did a good job," say, "You're becoming someone who takes responsibility." Instead of "You're so smart," say, "You're the kind of person who loves figuring things out." These statements link effort to character, not just performance. Over time, they build internal standards instead of dependence on praise.

The Social Mirror

Identity doesn't form in isolation; it's built in conversation with others. During adolescence, peers become powerful mirrors. What friends value starts to shape what feels valuable. Belonging signals safety, and safety frees the brain to grow. But belonging can also trap motivation if it depends on approval instead of authenticity.

Social media amplifies this tension. Online spaces offer validation at lightning speed, but they also encourage performance over self-discovery. Teens begin to ask, "Who am I?" and hear the echo: "Who do others want me to be?" The constant comparison can blur the line between authentic identity and curated image.

Adults can help by anchoring conversations in real values, not appearances. Ask questions that point inward rather than outward: "What kind of person do you respect most?" "When do you feel most yourself?" "What are you proud of when no one's watching?" These prompts guide attention back to the internal compass that drives sustainable motivation.

Identity Through Action

Identity doesn't grow from thinking alone — it grows from *doing*. Each time young people act in alignment with their values, they strengthen the neural connections that define who they are. Want to help a teen see themselves as compassionate? Give them opportunities to help others. Want them to see themselves as capable? Let them lead, even in small ways.

Experience precedes confidence. When a student teaches a peer or finishes a tough project, they're not just building skills — they're rewriting their self-story: "I can do hard things." That story, more than any reward or punishment, predicts future motivation. Once effort feels like part of identity, it becomes self-sustaining.

Supporting the Search

Adults often feel tempted to rescue young people from confusion, but it's better to accompany them through it. Offer perspective without prescribing answers. Share your own turning points — moments when you doubted yourself and discovered who you were becoming. Vulnerability makes guidance credible. It says, "You're allowed to be unfinished."

Here are a few ways to nurture identity-driven motivation:

1. Encourage reflection through journaling or conversation.

2. Expose them to diverse experiences — travel, volunteering, art, nature — that let them test values in real contexts.

3. Affirm progress, not perfection. Identity is built from trial and error, not from getting everything right.

4. Model authenticity yourself. When adults act from their own values, they give permission for young people to do the same.

The Takeaway

Motivation doesn't come from telling young people what to do; it comes from helping them discover who they are. When they see effort as an expression of identity, discipline stops feeling like duty and starts feeling like purpose. They move from asking, "Do I have to?" to saying, "This is who I am."

A strong identity is the foundation for lasting motivation. It gives every choice meaning and every challenge direction. Our role is not to define it for them, but to create the safety, curiosity, and encouragement that let it emerge. When we do, young people stop trying to live up to someone else's expectations — and start growing into their own.

Chapter 6 — The Purpose Path

Guiding Young People to Connect Goals with Meaning

Ask a teenager why they're studying for a test, and you might hear, "Because I have to," or, "So my parents won't yell at me." Rarely will you hear, "Because I want to understand the world," or "Because I see how this fits into my future." Yet purpose — the sense that effort connects to something larger and meaningful — is the true engine of motivation.

Young people are not born lazy; they're born searching. Between 10 and 25, they are building not only knowledge but *direction*. They're trying to answer the question, "What am I doing this for?" Helping them find that answer is one of the most powerful things any adult can do.

The Need for Meaning

Human beings are wired to look for purpose. The brain releases dopamine not only for immediate rewards but also for progress toward meaningful goals. When we feel our actions matter, effort feels good. When effort feels pointless, even small tasks feel heavy.

Adolescents live in a world overflowing with stimuli but short on meaning. They're told what to study, how to behave, what to achieve — but rarely *why*. Without that connection, motivation turns mechanical: enough to get through, not enough to thrive.

Purpose brings coherence to chaos. It turns random effort into a story — one in which the young person is not a passenger but a protagonist.

How Purpose Develops

Purpose doesn't arrive as a revelation; it unfolds gradually. Psychologist William Damon describes it as "a stable intention to accomplish something meaningful to the self and consequential to the world." For young people, purpose often starts small — an interest, a spark, a curiosity — and deepens through experience.

The early teenage years are about exploration. A hobby, a cause, a favorite subject — these are clues. The mid- to late-teen years bring integration: "This matters to me because it connects with who I want to become." By the early twenties, purpose begins to stabilize, linking personal values with contributions to others.

Adults can nurture this process by exposing young people to diverse experiences and helping them notice what energizes them. Purpose grows best where curiosity meets contribution.

From Pressure to Purpose

Many adults try to motivate through pressure: "You need good grades to get into college," or "You'll never succeed if you don't work hard." Those statements may be true, but they speak to fear, not meaning. Fear might trigger short bursts of effort, but purpose sustains effort over time.

The shift happens when we connect achievement to identity and contribution. Instead of saying, "You need good grades," try, "Learning how to manage challenges now will give you freedom later." Instead of "You'll never succeed if you don't work hard," try, "Every skill you build now makes you more capable of shaping your own future."

Purpose reframes effort as empowerment, not obligation.

The Role of Contribution

Young people often find purpose when they realize they can make a difference. Volunteering, mentoring, creating art, or solving a problem that matters — these experiences transform abstract learning into lived impact.

Neuroscience supports this: acts of giving and contribution activate the brain's reward system just like receiving does.

Helping others produces a lasting sense of value that external rewards can't match.

Encouraging community projects, social action, or even small gestures of kindness helps adolescents see themselves as *agents*, not spectators. It answers the question, "Do I matter?" with a clear and embodied yes.

Questions That Unlock Purpose

Purpose can't be handed down, but it can be uncovered. Adults can spark reflection with simple, open-ended questions:

⇒ What kind of problems do you care about solving?

⇒ When do you feel most alive or absorbed in what you're doing?

⇒ Who inspires you, and why?

⇒ What would you love to improve about the world around you?

Even if a young person shrugs or jokes, the question lingers. The brain keeps working on it in the background. Over time, small moments of clarity begin to add up — a favorite teacher, a project that feels meaningful, a cause that stirs emotion. Those experiences form the foundation of purpose.

Helping Them See the Bigger Picture

Adults can model purpose by sharing their own. Talk about why your work matters to you, what keeps you going when things are hard, or what values guide your choices. Young people learn more from watching authentic purpose than from hearing speeches about it.

When a parent or teacher admits, "This is why I care about what I do," it gives permission for self-discovery. It turns abstract advice into lived example.

Purpose also grows in conversations about the future that focus not just on careers but on *impact*. Ask, "What kind of person do you want to be in your community?" rather than only, "What job do you want?" The first question connects to values; the second, to tasks.

Purpose in an Age of Distraction

Digital life can make purpose harder to find. The constant flow of content trains attention toward novelty, not depth. Young people may feel busy but empty — always consuming, rarely creating. Helping them slow down and reflect is a radical act.

Encourage "quiet spaces" — moments without screens, where they can think, dream, or simply be. Purpose doesn't appear in noise; it emerges in reflection.

The Takeaway

Purpose is the bridge between the present and the future. It gives young people a reason to persist through boredom, failure, and fear. Without it, even talented teens drift. With it, they endure, adapt, and grow.

Our role is not to assign purpose but to invite it — to show that every effort, however small, can matter. When young people feel that connection between who they are, what they value, and what they do, they stop chasing motivation and start living it.

When they discover their *why*, the *how* takes care of itself

Part II

The Social World That Shapes Motivation

Chapter 7 — Motivation Starts at Home

Parenting Approaches That Inspire Confidence and Independence

Every parent wants their child to grow up motivated, confident, and responsible. Yet, many homes turn into battlefields over unfinished homework, messy rooms, and endless reminders. Parents plead, nag, threaten, reward—and still, motivation slips away. The question isn't whether parents care; it's how their approach shapes the inner drive of their children.

Home is the first motivational classroom. Long before teachers or bosses appear, the family environment teaches lessons about effort, confidence, and self-worth. How parents respond to success, failure, and struggle forms a blueprint for how young people approach challenges for the rest of their lives.

The Emotional Climate of Motivation

Children and teens learn motivation not from lectures but from *atmosphere*. When the home feels like a place of safety and respect, the brain stays open to learning. When it feels like a place of pressure or judgment, the brain switches to defense mode.

Neuroscience shows that chronic criticism or comparison activates the brain's stress response, flooding it with cortisol and narrowing focus to survival, not growth. On the other hand, warmth combined with structure—what psychologists call *authoritative parenting*—creates the ideal motivational environment: high expectations balanced by emotional support.

Authoritarian styles ("Do it because I said so") can produce obedience but rarely initiative. Permissive styles ("Do whatever you want") may feel kind but offer no framework for discipline. The sweet spot is guidance with trust. "I believe in you, and I'll help you figure this out" communicates faith and partnership rather than control.

Connection Before Correction

When a young person feels disconnected, motivation collapses. Before they'll listen to advice, they need to feel seen. Connection activates cooperation. Correction without connection, however, triggers rebellion or withdrawal.

Start by replacing interrogation with curiosity. Instead of "Why didn't you finish your work?" try "What made

it   hard   to   focus   tonight?"
Instead of "You need to care more," try "What part of this feels pointless to you?"

These small shifts turn arguments into conversations. They also send a deeper message: "Your perspective matters." When young people feel respected, they become more willing to take responsibility for their own effort.

Encouragement vs. Praise

Parents often confuse encouragement with praise. Praise focuses on outcome—"You're so smart," "You're the best." Encouragement focuses on process—"You worked hard on that," "I like how you stuck with it."

Outcome praise can feel good in the moment but creates dependency. It ties self-worth to success and fear to failure. Encouragement, by contrast, builds resilience. It tells the young person that what matters most is effort and learning.

Encouragement also models realistic optimism. Instead of saying, "You can do anything," which may feel untrue, say, "You can learn to do hard things." That message builds grit instead of perfectionism.

The Role of Autonomy at Home

Motivation thrives on a sense of control. Parents who allow appropriate choices teach responsibility better than those who micromanage every decision. Even small choices—what to wear, when to study, how to organize a task—signal trust.

Offering choices within boundaries works best: "You can do your homework before dinner or after, but it needs to be done today." "You can spend your allowance how you like, as long as you save part of it."

This combination of freedom and structure mirrors real life. It gives young people practice balancing independence with accountability—the foundation of adult motivation.

Modeling Motivation

Children learn what motivation looks like by watching it. Parents who pursue their own goals with curiosity and persistence teach more than any speech ever could. When they see you reading, learning, or handling setbacks calmly, they internalize that behavior as normal.

Be honest about your struggles, too. Saying, "I didn't feel like working out today, but I did it anyway because it helps me feel strong," teaches discipline without preaching. It shows that motivation isn't constant—it's something adults also cultivate intentionally.

The Power of Repair

No parent gets this right all the time. Everyone loses patience or says things in frustration. What matters is what happens next. Repair—apologizing, acknowledging feelings, and starting fresh—builds trust and models emotional maturity.

When a parent says, "I was too harsh earlier. I know you're trying, and I should have listened more," it teaches humility, accountability, and empathy—all traits that reinforce intrinsic motivation.

Repair tells the child, "We can recover." That message becomes a life skill.

Creating a Motivational Home Culture

A motivational home isn't one filled with pressure or perfectionism—it's one where effort is valued, curiosity is celebrated, and setbacks are treated as part of growth. Try these guiding principles:

1. Talk about effort more than results. Make hard work a shared value.

2.   Ask open questions. "What are you proud of today?" invites reflection.

3.   Keep curiosity alive. Encourage exploration, even if it's messy or unconventional.

4.   Share your own learning. Let them see you grow and change.

5.   Celebrate progress, not performance. Progress builds self-belief; performance builds anxiety.

Motivation is contagious. When young people see adults who find joy in effort and meaning in growth, they absorb that energy.

The Takeaway

Motivation starts with relationship, not regulation. At home, it grows in the quiet moments of trust, the small freedoms, the gentle words that say, "I believe in you." Parents don't have to be perfect—they only need to be present, curious, and consistent.

When love and structure coexist, the home becomes a place where young people learn the most valuable lesson of all: they are capable of shaping their own drive.

And once they believe that, they'll carry it into every classroom, every challenge, and every dream that follows.

Chapter 8 — Attachment, Safety, and Self-Drive

How Emotional Security Unlocks Motivation

Before motivation, there must be safety. Before curiosity, there must be trust. A young person cannot explore, take risks, or persist through difficulty if their mind is preoccupied with fear, shame, or uncertainty about belonging. The roots of drive are emotional, not mechanical — and they begin in relationships of security.

A confident teenager standing up for their ideas in class and a young adult persevering through failure both rely on an invisible foundation: the belief that they are loved and accepted, even when they stumble. That belief grows from *attachment*, the bond that forms between a child and their caregivers, and later extends to teachers, mentors, and peers. Motivation cannot bloom without it.

Why Safety Comes First

The brain's motivational systems are intertwined with its threat systems. When the brain senses danger — whether physical or emotional — it shifts resources from learning to protection. The amygdala, our internal alarm, floods the body with stress hormones like cortisol and adrenaline. Focus narrows, creativity shuts down, and the prefrontal cortex — the center of planning and self-control — temporarily goes offline.

In this state, reasoning, lecturing, or demanding effort doesn't work. The brain's first question is never "What should I do?" but "Am I safe?" Only when that answer is yes can motivation return.

Safety doesn't mean the absence of challenge. It means confidence that mistakes won't destroy connection. A teen who knows that a bad grade or a poor decision won't cost them love or respect is far more likely to keep trying.

The Secure Base

Psychologist John Bowlby described a secure attachment as a "safe base from which to explore the world." Children who feel securely attached grow into adolescents who can take healthy risks, handle setbacks, and regulate emotion — all key components of motivation.

Insecure attachment, by contrast, teaches the brain to conserve energy, avoid failure, or seek approval at any cost. A teen who feels they must constantly prove their worth will work hard under pressure but burn out quickly. Another may avoid effort altogether, convinced it's safer not to try than to fail.

Parents and mentors build a secure base not through perfection but through consistency: showing up, listening, and keeping promises. Small gestures — remembering a detail from yesterday's conversation, offering calm presence after an argument — send the message, "You matter even when you struggle." That message rewires the brain for resilience.

Emotional Regulation and Motivation

Emotional security gives young people the tools to manage frustration, disappointment, and fear — emotions that often derail effort. A securely attached brain learns that emotions are signals, not threats. "I'm angry" becomes "I care about this," and "I'm nervous" becomes "This matters to me."

Adults can support this regulation by *naming feelings* rather than dismissing them. "I can see you're frustrated with this project" is far more helpful than "Calm down." Naming emotions activates the prefrontal cortex, helping the brain move from reaction to reflection. Over time, this practice teaches self-motivation: the ability to stay engaged even when things are hard.

Trust and the Freedom to Fail

Nothing kills motivation faster than the fear of failure. If every mistake brings judgment, the brain learns to hide rather than try. A culture of trust changes that equation. When adults respond to failure with empathy — "What did you learn?" instead of "What went wrong?" — they turn error into data, not danger.

In schools and families where mistakes are treated as part of growth, young people take more initiative. They innovate, ask questions, and take ownership of their progress. They stop working to avoid punishment and start working to discover possibility.

Relationships That Motivate

Every motivated young person has at least one adult who believes in them. Research on resilience calls this the "charismatic adult effect" — one stable, caring relationship that communicates, "You are capable." It might be a parent, teacher, coach, or mentor. That relationship acts as emotional armor, buffering stress and keeping the motivational system online.

Adults don't have to fix every problem. Simply being present — showing genuine interest, listening without rushing to solve — creates the psychological safety that allows growth. When a teen says, "You don't get it," what they often mean is, "I don't feel safe enough to be honest yet." Patience and empathy open that door.

Building a Culture of Safety

Emotional safety isn't just personal; it's cultural. Homes and classrooms that emphasize respect, inclusion, and predictability become motivational incubators. Clear boundaries provide stability; kindness provides courage. Together, they teach that effort is always worth the risk.

Practical ways to nurture this culture include:

1. Predictability: Keep routines and follow through on commitments. Consistency builds trust.

2. Empathy: Reflect emotions before offering advice. "That sounds disappointing" calms the nervous system.

3. Repair: After conflict, reconnect quickly. "I got upset earlier — let's start over."

4. Recognition: Notice small efforts. Feeling seen reinforces agency.

The Takeaway

Before young people can be self-driven, they must feel safe enough to drive. Emotional security is not a luxury; it's the fuel of motivation. It allows curiosity to replace fear and effort to replace avoidance.

A secure relationship doesn't eliminate struggle — it anchors it. When young people know they can fall without losing connection, they dare to climb higher. And that courage, more than any rule or reward, is what turns potential into purpose.

Chapter 9 — The Peer Effect

How Friendships and Belonging Shape Motivation

Ask any parent what influences their teenager most, and they'll usually sigh before answering: "Their friends." They're not wrong. From middle school onward, peers become the single most powerful social force in a young person's life. They can inspire excellence or distraction, confidence or insecurity, purpose or conformity. But beneath all the drama and intensity lies something deeper — a biological truth. The adolescent brain is wired for belonging.

Friendship during these years isn't just social; it's neurological. As young people transition from family dependence to independence, their brains reorganize around connection and acceptance. Motivation — what they choose to care about, work for, and believe in — is profoundly shaped by the people who surround them.

The Social Brain in Overdrive

Around puberty, the brain's *social reward system* lights up. Interactions with peers trigger dopamine surges similar to those caused by excitement or success. Acceptance feels euphoric; rejection feels painful — literally. Neuroimaging studies show that social exclusion activates the same regions as physical pain.

This heightened sensitivity isn't weakness; it's evolution. For early humans, belonging to a group meant survival. Adolescents today carry the same circuitry, but the "tribe" has expanded to include classrooms, teams, and digital communities. Every post, comment, or glance becomes a social signal: "Am I accepted?" "Do I matter here?"

Because of this, peer approval can become a stronger motivator than adult authority. A teen who won't complete homework for a teacher might stay up all night perfecting a group project because their friends depend on them. Motivation shifts from compliance to connection.

The Double-Edged Sword of Belonging

Belonging is one of the most powerful motivators — but it cuts both ways. When group values encourage growth, empathy, and integrity, peers can supercharge positive motivation. But when belonging depends on conformity, image, or risk-taking, the same system drives unhealthy behavior.

That's why prevention efforts that rely on fear ("Don't give in to peer pressure") often fail. The need for belonging is stronger than fear. The key isn't to eliminate peer influence but to shape the environment where it operates. If young people feel accepted by supportive, purpose-driven peers, they naturally resist negative pressures.

Healthy belonging protects against despair and disengagement. Isolation, by contrast, drains motivation. Teens who feel excluded often retreat into apathy or online worlds that simulate connection without real intimacy. The solution isn't cutting off screens or friends — it's helping them find communities that reflect their best selves.

Friendship as a Motivational Mirror

Friendships are mirrors in which young people see who they're becoming. When they're around peers who value effort, kindness, or creativity, those traits feel rewarding to express. When their circle dismisses ambition or mocks sincerity, motivation shrinks in self-defense.

Adults can gently help teens reflect on these dynamics without judgment. Ask, "How do you feel about yourself when you're with that group?" or "Who helps you be the version of yourself you like most?" These questions invite self-awareness instead of criticism.

Encouraging diversity in friendships also expands perspective. When teens interact with people from different backgrounds and interests, they discover new ways of thinking — and new reasons to care. Motivation grows when identity expands beyond one social circle.

The Role of Mentorship and Peer Leadership

Peers don't just influence each other horizontally; influence can flow upward too. Older students, youth leaders, and mentors act as "near peers" — models close enough to be relatable but far enough ahead to inspire. A high school senior mentoring a younger student has more motivational power than most adults precisely because they speak the same social language.

Programs that pair youth in mentorship roles consistently show boosts in engagement and confidence for both sides. The mentor feels trusted and capable; the mentee feels seen and supported. Both experience the dopamine rush of belonging through contribution rather than performance.

Social Media and the Illusion of Connection

In the digital age, belonging has migrated online. Social media can offer connection but also breeds comparison. The highlight reels of others' lives can distort self-worth and motivation, making authentic effort feel invisible.

Still, digital spaces aren't the enemy; they're extensions of the same social instincts. Teaching digital self-awareness — noticing how certain interactions make them feel — helps young people reclaim agency. "Do you feel energized or drained after being online?" is a simple but powerful question. When they learn to recognize emotional signals, they start curating digital spaces that motivate rather than demoralize.

Creating Communities That Inspire

Adults can foster environments — at home, in schools, or in sports — that channel the peer effect toward growth rather than pressure. A few guiding principles:

1. Encourage collaboration over competition. Shared goals create bonds that amplify motivation.

2. Highlight teamwork. Publicly recognize when students or siblings support each other.

3. Model inclusion. Celebrate difference and discourage cliques or exclusionary jokes.

4. Support positive peer leadership. Give teens real influence — not just responsibility — within their groups.

Belonging doesn't require everyone to be alike; it requires everyone to feel valued.

The Takeaway

Motivation doesn't grow in isolation. It spreads through connection, imitation, and shared emotion. Every friendship, team, and group chat teaches young people what effort is worth. The question isn't whether peers will shape motivation — they will — but how we can help them do it wisely.

When belonging meets purpose, the peer effect becomes a force for growth. Young people push each other higher, not because adults demand it, but because they want to rise together. And in that shared climb, they discover something lasting: that the energy of connection can move mountains that individual willpower never could.

Chapter 10 — Social Media and the Attention Economy

Helping Youth Stay Motivated in a Distracting World

For many young people, social media isn't a pastime — it's the background of daily life. They scroll while eating breakfast, chat between classes, and check notifications before bed. It connects them, entertains them, and shapes how they see themselves. But it also competes for the very thing motivation depends on most: attention.

Motivation begins with focus. Without the ability to sustain attention on what matters, even the most ambitious goals dissolve into noise. The challenge for today's youth isn't a lack of desire to succeed — it's living in an environment engineered to hijack their motivation systems.

The Science of the Scroll

Every swipe, click, and notification on social media is designed to trigger dopamine, the brain's "wanting" chemical. Platforms use unpredictable rewards — likes, messages, new posts — to keep users engaged in a loop of anticipation. It's the same mechanism that keeps gamblers at slot machines.

For the adolescent brain, this system is especially powerful. Between 10 and 25, dopamine sensitivity is at its peak. The brain learns through novelty and social feedback, both of which social media delivers in endless supply. Each notification feels like a small spark of significance — *someone sees me.*

But the cost of that constant stimulation is attention fragmentation. The brain adapts to rapid switching, making it harder to stay focused on slower, effortful tasks like reading, problem-solving, or reflecting. Over time, real-world rewards — grades, hobbies, relationships — can feel less stimulating than digital ones.

The Illusion of Connection

Social media gives the appearance of belonging, but often without the depth that sustains motivation. Online interactions can amplify comparison, anxiety, and perfectionism. Teens see peers achieving, traveling, or succeeding, and feel an unspoken question: *Why not me?*

That comparison can quietly erode intrinsic motivation. Instead of doing things for enjoyment or growth, young people start doing them for validation — likes, comments, or recognition. When attention replaces meaning as the goal, drive becomes fragile.

Yet social media isn't inherently harmful. It can foster community, creativity, and learning — when used intentionally. The difference lies in agency: is the young person controlling the tool, or is the tool controlling them?

Attention as a Skill

Attention isn't fixed; it's trainable. Teaching young people to manage focus is one of the most valuable life skills of the modern era. It starts with awareness: noticing when and why attention drifts.

Ask them to reflect: "When you're online, what kinds of posts make you feel inspired? Which ones make you feel drained?" These questions activate the prefrontal cortex — the brain's regulation center — and help transform automatic scrolling into conscious choice.

Encourage "attention training" practices:

⇒ Single-tasking. Do one thing at a time — study, listen, or relax — without multitasking.

⇒ Screen breaks. Five minutes outdoors or away from devices resets dopamine levels.

⇒ Mindful pauses. Before opening an app, take a breath and ask, "What am I looking for right now?"

These habits rebuild the neural circuits that support focus and intrinsic motivation.

Reclaiming Meaning in the Digital World

The antidote to distraction isn't total disconnection — it's *reconnection* to meaning. Help young people link digital activity to their real-world goals and values. A teen passionate about music might use social platforms to share songs or connect with other creators. A student interested in social justice might follow organizations that inspire offline action.

Encouraging purposeful use gives social media back its potential as a motivational tool instead of a drain. The question shifts from "How much time are you online?" to "What are you using it for?"

Adults can model this, too. When parents and teachers treat their own devices mindfully — putting phones away during meals, talking about boundaries, or sharing what they've learned from online experiences — they normalize digital discipline rather than digital shame.

The Digital Detox Myth

There's a common belief that motivation will return if teens simply quit social media. While short breaks can help reset attention, long-term motivation requires balance, not withdrawal. Social connection is a developmental need, and digital platforms are often the main space where that need is met. The goal is to help young people develop *digital maturity*: the ability to use technology consciously, critically, and creatively.

You can guide this by encouraging "intentional scrolling." Suggest they follow people who inspire learning, creativity, or compassion — not just entertainment. Ask them to create before they consume: post something meaningful, learn a new skill, write a reflection. Creation activates the brain's reward centers differently, reinforcing agency instead of passivity.

Protecting the Brain's Quiet

One of the most powerful ways to sustain motivation is to protect moments of quiet. The brain needs downtime to consolidate memories, generate insight, and restore focus. Encourage digital "white space": no screens before bed, reading time without devices, or simple moments of stillness.

Silence and boredom aren't enemies of motivation — they're its soil. In those quiet gaps, the brain connects ideas, imagines possibilities, and rehearses goals.

The Takeaway

Social media isn't destroying motivation; it's competing for it. The same neural systems that make young people curious, creative, and socially driven are being constantly stimulated by design. But when they learn to manage attention — to scroll with awareness, to connect with purpose, and to protect mental space — they reclaim control over the very chemistry that fuels motivation.

The digital world will only grow louder. Helping youth stay motivated isn't about pulling them away from it, but about teaching them how to listen inwardly amid the noise. When they can do that, focus becomes freedom — and freedom becomes the foundation of lasting drive.

Chapter 11 — School Motivation 101

Why Traditional Education Often Kills Curiosity

Walk into most classrooms today, and you'll see students quietly taking notes, filling in worksheets, or memorizing material for an upcoming test. On the surface, everything looks fine — structured, productive, even efficient. But beneath that calm order, something essential is often missing: *curiosity.*

Curiosity is the engine of motivation. It's what makes young people explore, question, and persist. Yet, for many, school slowly replaces curiosity with compliance. The same students who once asked endless questions in elementary school now stare blankly at the clock, waiting for the bell to ring. It's not that they've lost their desire to learn — it's that the system has trained it out of them.

The Problem of External Motivation

Traditional education still operates largely on extrinsic motivators: grades, rewards, punishment, and comparison. Students are told to study for the test, raise their GPA, or earn a spot in a good university. The message is clear — learning isn't valuable for its own sake; it's a means to an end.

Neuroscience shows that extrinsic pressure activates stress circuits in the brain, narrowing focus and reducing creativity. In contrast, intrinsic motivation — learning driven by interest and meaning — lights up the brain's reward networks, releasing dopamine and promoting deeper engagement. When students are learning out of curiosity rather than fear, the brain literally functions better.

The irony is that education's goal is to create lifelong learners, yet many students leave school believing learning is something you endure, not enjoy.

The Curiosity Crisis

Children enter school with boundless curiosity. They ask "why" about everything. But as they grow older, the emphasis shifts from exploration to evaluation. The right answer becomes more important than the interesting question. Mistakes, once a natural part of discovery, become something to avoid.

Curiosity thrives in uncertainty — in the space between what we know and what we want to know. But standardized education often eliminates that space. The structure rewards conformity, not wonder. The question isn't "What fascinates you?" but "What's on the exam?"

This approach suppresses the brain's natural reward system. When learning feels imposed, dopamine drops. Without that spark, focus fades, and students start relying on external rewards — praise, grades, or approval — to keep going. Over time, they learn to play the game of school rather than the game of learning.

Mistakes as Motivation

One of the most damaging myths in education is that mistakes equal failure. In reality, error is the raw material of mastery. Neuroscience shows that the brain grows most when it detects and corrects errors. Every "wrong" answer triggers a feedback loop that refines understanding.

Unfortunately, many classrooms treat mistakes as evidence of weakness rather than as steps toward growth. Students learn to hide confusion or avoid risk. But when educators normalize mistakes as data — information that guides progress — motivation and confidence rise together.

Creating a culture where it's safe to fail doesn't mean lowering standards. It means reframing effort as exploration. The best teachers turn every misstep into a chance for reflection: "What did you notice? What might you try next?" That's where curiosity reignites.

The Role of Autonomy in Learning

The adolescent brain craves autonomy — the freedom to choose and create. Yet, school often limits choice to the smallest details: where to sit, when to speak, what to memorize. This lack of ownership quietly kills engagement.

Students are more motivated when they have a say in what or how they learn. Even small amounts of choice — selecting a project topic, setting personal goals, or designing part of an assignment — can transform apathy into energy. Autonomy doesn't require abandoning structure; it means trusting students enough to give them responsibility.

When young people feel that their voice matters, their brain's motivation circuits activate. The same dopamine system that drives them toward social media or hobbies can drive them toward learning — if they experience ownership.

Relationships and Relevance

Research consistently shows that the most important factor in student motivation isn't technology, curriculum, or class size — it's the *relationship* between teacher and student. When young people feel known and respected, they try harder. Connection creates safety, and safety fuels curiosity.

Equally vital is relevance. When students see how learning connects to real life, engagement deepens. Algebra becomes meaningful when linked to building or budgeting. Literature comes alive when discussed through the lens of modern culture or personal identity. The brain learns best when it can connect new knowledge to something that already matters.

The Way Forward

Rebuilding motivation in schools means restoring curiosity to its rightful place at the center of learning. That requires shifting from a culture of performance to a culture of exploration — one where questions are valued as much as answers.

Here's what helps:

1. Encourage inquiry. Let students ask and pursue their own questions, not just answer yours.

2. Reward process, not just results. Celebrate persistence, creativity, and growth.

3. Make learning social. Collaboration transforms effort into shared discovery.

4. Give room for choice. Even small decisions can build ownership and pride.

5.   Connect to purpose. Link lessons to real-world issues, passions, or values.

The Takeaway

Schools were meant to be gardens for curiosity, not factories for grades. When we treat learning as a human adventure rather than a checklist, motivation returns naturally.

Young people want to learn — their brains are built for it. Our job is to remove the barriers that make them forget that truth. When curiosity is rekindled, effort stops being forced and becomes joyful again. And in that joy lies the spark that education was always meant to ignite.

Chapter 12 — Reigniting the Joy of Learning

How Teachers Can Design Classrooms That Spark Engagement

If curiosity is the flame of learning, then the teacher is its keeper. Every day, educators stand at the intersection of science and soul — balancing curriculum goals with the deeper mission of awakening minds. Yet in many schools, the spark has dimmed. Students show up physically but not mentally, moving through lessons like passengers on autopilot. The challenge for today's teacher isn't transferring knowledge; it's reigniting *wonder*.

Motivation thrives where students feel safe to explore, excited to participate, and trusted to think. The question is no longer "How do we make them learn?" but "How do we help them *want* to learn again?"

The Emotional Climate of the Classroom

The brain learns best in a climate of emotional safety. When students fear embarrassment, judgment, or failure, the stress hormone cortisol rises, suppressing curiosity and memory. In contrast, positive emotions — interest, playfulness, laughter —

release dopamine and serotonin, strengthening attention and recall.

Creating safety doesn't mean removing rigor. It means building trust. Students must believe that mistakes won't lead to humiliation, and that their voices matter. Simple gestures — greeting them by name, acknowledging effort, or showing genuine enthusiasm — communicate respect and belonging. These cues tell the brain, "It's safe to think here."

A classroom rooted in warmth and high expectations becomes a motivational ecosystem: supportive enough for risk-taking, structured enough for focus.

From Compliance to Curiosity

Many students have learned to treat education as performance — answer the question, get the grade, move on. To break that pattern, teachers can reintroduce the spirit of discovery. Begin with inquiry rather than instruction: "What do you notice about this?" "Why do you think that happens?" "What would you change if you could?"

Questions like these spark cognitive ownership. When students generate ideas, they activate the same reward circuits that drive gaming or problem-solving. The brain loves puzzles more than lectures.

One effective approach is the "curiosity hook" — starting a lesson with something unexpected: a mystery photo, a short story, a surprising statistic. These small moments of novelty release dopamine and prime the brain for learning. Once curiosity is engaged, even complex material becomes easier to absorb.

Relevance Is Motivation

Relevance is the bridge between the classroom and the real world. When students can connect lessons to their lives, motivation deepens. A math problem about abstract numbers might seem dull, but turn it into a design challenge for a skateboard ramp or a budgeting exercise for a trip, and interest grows.

Teachers can enhance relevance by connecting curriculum topics to current events, social issues, or student interests. Literature classes come alive when students link themes to modern music or media. Science classes flourish when framed around questions like, "How does this affect our planet?" or "How could this improve lives?"

Relevance gives meaning to effort. It transforms "I have to learn this" into "I want to understand this."

The Power of Choice

Choice is one of the simplest yet most powerful motivational tools. Allowing students even minor decisions — selecting essay topics, choosing partners, designing experiments — communicates trust and autonomy. When they feel ownership over learning, engagement skyrockets.

Choice doesn't mean chaos. Teachers can offer structured options: two project formats, three discussion prompts, or a menu of creative ways to demonstrate understanding. This sense of agency activates the prefrontal cortex, the part of the brain responsible for planning and persistence.

When students feel like partners in learning, they stop working for approval and start working for pride.

Collaboration and Community

Learning is social by nature. When classrooms emphasize collaboration over competition, motivation shifts from individual survival to collective success. Group projects, peer teaching, and shared reflection create environments where students feel accountable to one another, not just to the teacher.

Well-designed collaboration fosters empathy, communication, and curiosity. A struggling student might persist longer when teammates depend on them. A high-achieving student might rediscover joy by helping others succeed. Motivation multiplies when it's shared.

Teachers can nurture this by recognizing cooperative effort publicly: "I loved how you supported each other in solving that problem." It sends the message that learning together *matters*.

Feedback That Fuels Growth

Traditional grading often signals the end of learning: a score, a judgment, a period at the end of a sentence. But feedback can be a beginning instead — a catalyst for growth.

Effective feedback is specific, timely, and focused on process rather than personality. "Your argument is clear — now strengthen the evidence here," builds confidence and direction. Praise effort, but also guide next steps. The goal is to keep the learning loop alive: try, reflect, improve.

When students view feedback as collaboration instead of evaluation, they become more resilient. Each correction becomes information, not criticism.

Reimagining the Role of the Teacher

In the motivational classroom, the teacher is not the keeper of answers but the designer of experiences. Their power lies not in authority but in inspiration. The best educators act like mentors and facilitators — balancing structure with spontaneity, guiding curiosity without smothering it.

They remind students that learning isn't about perfection; it's about progress. They model curiosity themselves — asking questions, admitting when they don't know, and showing that learning never ends.

The Takeaway

Reigniting the joy of learning doesn't require new technology or endless innovation. It begins with seeing students not as test-takers, but as thinkers in progress. When classrooms become places of curiosity, relevance, and emotional safety, motivation returns naturally.

The goal of education has never been just to fill minds, but to *ignite* them. When teachers create spaces where curiosity feels safe and success feels personal, students rediscover what every child once knew instinctively — that learning is one of life's greatest pleasures.

Part III

Building Grit, Growth, and Self-Mastery

Chapter 13 — What Grit Really Is

Why Persistence Isn't Personality — It's Trainable

Every generation looks at the next and worries that they've become softer. "Kids today give up too easily," adults say, watching teens abandon projects or switch interests as quickly as they scroll screens. But the truth is more complex. Grit — the ability to stay focused through discomfort and delay — isn't something you're born with or without. It's something that grows.

Persistence is not a personality trait; it's a skill shaped by environment, mindset, and experience. And just like any other skill, it can be strengthened with the right conditions — safety, support, and purpose.

The Real Meaning of Grit

Psychologist Angela Duckworth popularized the term *grit* as a combination of passion and perseverance toward long-term goals. Grit is not stubbornness or blind endurance. It's commitment to growth over time. It means caring about something deeply enough to keep going, even when it's boring, uncomfortable, or uncertain.

Grit doesn't ignore failure — it learns from it. It doesn't deny frustration — it manages it. And it isn't about working endlessly; it's about sustaining meaningful effort.

The key insight from Duckworth's research is that gritty individuals aren't the ones who never feel like quitting. They're the ones who've learned how to keep moving anyway.

Why Young People Struggle With Persistence

The modern world makes persistence harder than ever. The teenage brain's sensitivity to novelty means new opportunities — new hobbies, new videos, new conversations — are always more rewarding than the familiar grind. Technology magnifies that impulse, offering instant dopamine hits for minimal effort.

At the same time, many young people grow up in systems that emphasize performance over process. They're rewarded for outcomes, not persistence. They learn that success equals talent, not time — a message that makes failure feel fatal.

When a student thinks, "If I were smart, this would be easy," they're more likely to give up at the first obstacle. But when they think, "Struggle means I'm learning," persistence rises naturally. The difference is mindset, not willpower.

The Growth Mindset Connection

Psychologist Carol Dweck's *growth mindset* theory complements grit perfectly. A fixed mindset says, "I'm good or bad at this." A growth mindset says, "I can get better at this." The second approach builds endurance because it reframes effort as evidence of progress, not proof of weakness.

Every time adults praise effort instead of outcome, they reinforce this belief. "You worked hard on that problem," creates grit. "You're so smart," erodes it. The first message tells the brain that improvement is possible. The second traps it in fear of losing approval.

Young people with a growth mindset are more likely to recover from setbacks, seek feedback, and stay motivated through difficulty. Grit is the visible result of that invisible belief.

The Role of Purpose in Persistence

Grit needs a reason. No one pushes through discomfort for a goal that feels meaningless. The most resilient young people tie their effort to a sense of purpose — whether it's mastering a skill, helping others, or proving something to themselves.

Adults can help them find that connection. Instead of saying, "Don't quit," ask, "Why did you start?" or "What would it feel like to finish?" These questions shift attention from pain to purpose, reactivating motivation.

Purpose turns willpower into passion. When young people understand *why* something matters, perseverance feels less like punishment and more like pride.

Teaching Grit Gently

Contrary to popular belief, grit isn't built through toughness or deprivation. It grows in environments that balance challenge with support.

1. Model perseverance. Let young people see you struggle and persist. "This was hard for me, but I kept at it," is powerful modeling.

2. Normalize frustration. Teach that feeling stuck doesn't mean failure — it means growth is happening.

3. Break down big goals. Small, consistent wins wire the brain for persistence. Each success releases dopamine, building momentum.

4. Reflect on progress. Help them notice improvement. Reflection turns effort into evidence of ability.

Compassion, not pressure, builds true grit. When young people feel safe enough to fail, they stop avoiding challenge and start embracing it.

When to Let Go

Sometimes quitting isn't weakness — it's wisdom. Grit is not about clinging to every commitment forever. It's about knowing when to persist and when to pivot. Teaching discernment is part of teaching resilience.

Ask, "Is this goal still meaningful to you?" or "Are you quitting because it's hard or because it's not aligned with who you are?" These reflections teach young people to separate temporary frustration from genuine redirection.

Real grit includes the courage to change paths — not out of fear, but out of clarity.

The Takeaway

Grit isn't a character test; it's a developmental process. It grows when adults model patience, celebrate effort, and connect struggle to meaning. It weakens when we equate toughness with worth or treat failure as shame.

Young people don't need to be hardened — they need to be guided. When they learn that persistence isn't about perfection but progress, they stop fearing the grind and start trusting the process.

And that trust, more than any lecture or reward, is what turns short bursts of motivation into a lifetime of resilience.

Chapter 14 — How to Teach Grit and Self-Regulation

Practical Methods to Build Focus and Follow-Through

Everyone wants young people to be resilient — to stick with hard things, stay calm under pressure, and finish what they start. Yet we rarely teach them *how* to do it. We say, "Don't give up," or "Stay focused," but those are outcomes, not skills. Grit and self-regulation aren't magic traits; they're trainable abilities that grow through practice, reflection, and encouragement.

What Self-Regulation Really Means

Self-regulation is the ability to manage attention, emotion, and behavior in pursuit of a goal. It's the invisible muscle behind motivation. A teen who can delay gratification, plan steps, and recover from setbacks will outperform raw talent every time.

The brain's regulatory systems — housed mainly in the prefrontal cortex — continue developing into the mid-twenties. That means young people are still learning how to balance impulse and intention. Their emotional "accelerator" is strong, but the cognitive "brakes" are still maturing. Teaching regulation is like teaching them how to drive their own mind —

when to slow down, when to push forward, and how to steer back on course.

Practice Over Pressure

You can't force self-control through punishment or lectures. What works is *practice in small doses* — repeated opportunities to face manageable challenges and recover from them.

1. Micro-challenges. Encourage short tasks that stretch but don't overwhelm — studying for 20 minutes, finishing one chore, or running one extra lap. Each success rewires the brain's reward system to link effort with satisfaction.

2. Reflection. After effort, ask, "What helped you stick with it?" or "What distracted you?" Reflection strengthens awareness — the foundation of self-regulation.

3. Incremental goals. Break large projects into smaller milestones. Achieving these steps releases dopamine, keeping motivation alive.

4. Flexible routines. Teach consistency, but allow adaptation. Self-regulation grows through balance, not rigidity.

Pressure breeds avoidance; practice builds capacity.

Managing Emotion, Not Erasing It

Many adults tell kids to "calm down," "focus," or "stop overreacting." But emotions aren't the enemy of self-regulation — they're the data. Learning to name, interpret, and channel emotions is what gives grit its emotional intelligence.

Help young people translate feeling into focus:

> ⇒ "You're frustrated because you care about this — that's good energy."

> ⇒ "You're nervous because this matters to you — let's use that energy to prepare."

When adults validate emotions before problem-solving, the brain's alarm system quiets down, allowing the prefrontal cortex to reengage. The lesson becomes: *I can feel things and still stay in control.* That's the heart of resilience.

The Power of Recovery

Self-regulation isn't just about staying on task — it's about how you respond when you fall off. Everyone loses focus or motivation sometimes. What separates resilient learners from discouraged ones is the ability to *recover quickly.*

Model recovery yourself. Say, "I got distracted earlier, so I'm resetting my plan," or "That didn't go as I hoped — what can I learn for next time?" Normalizing recovery removes shame and teaches that consistency matters more than perfection.

Encourage "reset rituals" — brief, mindful actions that help refocus. A short walk, deep breaths, stretching, or writing down a next step can restart momentum. Over time, these rituals become internal habits of self-correction.

The Role of Adults as Coaches

Young people build self-regulation best when adults act as coaches, not controllers. Coaching means observing effort, asking reflective questions, and guiding rather than dictating.

Instead of saying, "You need to focus," try:

⇒ "What's making it hard to focus right now?"

⇒ "What's one thing you can do to make this easier?"

⇒ "How did you get back on track last time?"

This approach promotes *metacognition* — awareness of one's own thinking. When teens learn to analyze how their attention works, they begin managing it independently.

Coaching also means celebrating effort publicly and quietly supporting struggle privately. When adults respond with calm encouragement, they model emotional control. The tone becomes contagious.

Building Grit Through Meaningful Challenge

Grit doesn't grow from comfort; it grows from meaningful struggle. But "meaningful" is key — the task must matter to the learner. Encourage young people to set self-directed goals that align with their interests. Whether it's learning an instrument, coding a game, or training for a race, personal relevance fuels persistence.

Then, guide them through the *grind*. Break progress into measurable steps, and help them visualize success: "Each day you practice, you're building strength for your future self." Pair this with feedback that focuses on growth, not outcome. The message becomes, "You're getting stronger," not "You're still behind."

The Long Game of Self-Regulation

Like physical exercise, the benefits of self-regulation compound over time. Every moment of delayed gratification, every calm breath in frustration, every finished task is a neural repetition — a workout for the prefrontal cortex.

The goal isn't to eliminate distraction or emotion, but to create flexibility: the ability to notice, pause, and choose. Once young people experience that control — that they can direct their own mind — confidence and motivation surge.

The Takeaway

Grit and self-regulation are the twin engines of lasting motivation. They don't come from talent, toughness, or luck. They come from daily practice, compassionate coaching, and environments that make growth safe.

When we teach young people how to steer their own focus, handle their emotions, and persist through challenge, we give them more than discipline — we give them freedom. And freedom, more than fear or reward, is what keeps the human spirit moving forward.

Chapter 15 — The Science of Feedback

How Praise, Criticism, and Guidance Shape Motivation

Every word we say to a young person teaches them something about who they are — and what they're capable of becoming. Feedback is one of the most powerful tools in shaping motivation, yet it's often misunderstood. Some adults avoid giving it altogether for fear of discouraging, while others deliver it so bluntly that it shuts a young person down. The truth lies in between: feedback that is honest *and* supportive, specific *and* hopeful.

The way feedback is given can either ignite self-belief or extinguish it. Neuroscience confirms this — our brains respond differently to feedback depending on how it's framed. The right kind of response activates the brain's learning centers, while harsh criticism triggers its threat systems. Understanding this science can transform how we help young people grow.

Why Feedback Matters So Much

Feedback is more than evaluation; it's communication about potential. During adolescence, the brain is still mapping its self-image. Each piece of feedback becomes a clue in that map: "Am I competent?" "Am I valued?" "Should I keep trying?"

Constructive feedback fuels learning because it focuses on *process*, not identity. It says, "You can improve this," instead of, "You're good or bad at this." When young people interpret mistakes as opportunities to learn, motivation rises. When they interpret them as verdicts, motivation collapses.

Research shows that students who receive clear, process-oriented feedback outperform those who get only grades or generic praise. It's not the amount of feedback that matters — it's the *quality* and *tone*.

The Brain on Praise and Criticism

Praise and criticism trigger very different neurochemical responses. Praise releases dopamine, the brain's reward chemical, making us want to repeat the behavior. But not all praise is equal. "You're so smart" gives a fleeting rush but creates pressure to stay perfect. "You worked hard on this" produces pride rooted in effort — a far more sustainable motivator.

Criticism, on the other hand, activates the brain's threat circuits. When feedback feels like attack, the amygdala hijacks attention. The person stops listening and starts defending. In that moment, no learning occurs.

However, *constructive correction* — delivered with empathy and clarity — engages the prefrontal cortex instead. The brain interprets it as useful data, not danger. The difference isn't in the message itself but in *how it's given.*

The Ingredients of Effective Feedback

Good feedback balances truth with trust. It's grounded in respect, focused on growth, and framed as collaboration.

1. Be specific. "This paragraph is strong because you used evidence" teaches more than "Good job."

2. Start with what works. The brain hears the first thing you say most loudly. Begin with a strength before suggesting change.

3. Describe, don't label. "You interrupted twice during discussion" is more effective than "You're rude." Description invites reflection; labels trigger shame.

4. Offer a path forward. Feedback without guidance is just criticism. Always end with a next step: "Try breaking this problem into smaller parts next time."

This structure — *affirm, analyze, advise* — keeps communication balanced between encouragement and challenge.

The Role of Timing

Feedback works best when it's timely. The brain learns most efficiently when reflection follows action closely. Immediate feedback connects cause and effect; delayed feedback feels abstract.

That said, emotionally charged moments require space. If frustration or shame is high, waiting until calm returns prevents defensiveness. Timing isn't just about speed — it's about readiness. The best feedback meets the brain when it's open.

Creating a Feedback Culture

When feedback becomes part of the culture rather than a rare event, students and children stop fearing it. Teachers and parents can model this by asking for feedback themselves: "How did I explain that?" or "What could I do differently next time?" This humility turns feedback into a shared process of growth rather than a top-down judgment.

In classrooms, peer feedback can be powerful when guided properly. When students learn to offer constructive comments — "I liked how you structured this, maybe try adding more examples" — they strengthen empathy and critical thinking simultaneously. The goal is not to criticize but to help one another grow.

At home, families can practice similar habits during daily life. After group tasks or family discussions, reflect together: "What worked well? What can we improve next time?" Over time, feedback becomes normalized — not personal, but practical.

When Feedback Hurts

Even well-intentioned feedback can sting, especially for young people still forming self-esteem. The key is recovery. If a child reacts defensively, resist the urge to push harder. Instead, validate the emotion — "I can see that was hard to hear" — and revisit later with calm and care.

Never underestimate the power of repair. A brief follow-up — "I gave you a lot of feedback earlier because I believe in you" — restores trust and turns discomfort into growth. When young people know that feedback comes from belief, not disappointment, they listen differently.

From Judgment to Growth

The most powerful feedback doesn't judge who someone *is*; it guides who they can *become*. It's less about pointing out flaws and more about helping them see their own potential clearly.

When feedback is honest, kind, and actionable, it lights a path forward. It tells the developing brain: "You're capable of change." That belief is the seed of motivation.

The Takeaway

Feedback isn't a moment; it's a relationship. It works best when rooted in respect, curiosity, and shared purpose. When adults master the art of giving it — with warmth, timing, and specificity — young people stop fearing mistakes and start seeking growth.

In the end, great feedback is more than correction; it's connection. It says, "I see you trying, and I'm here to help you get better." And that message — far more than praise or criticism — is what turns effort into excellence.

Chapter 16 — From Perfectionism to Growth Mindset

Helping Young People See Failure as Part of Success

At first glance, perfectionism can look like motivation. The student who double-checks every answer, the athlete who trains obsessively, the young artist who erases and redraws the same line for hours — they all appear driven. But underneath that polish often lies fear: fear of failure, of disapproval, of not being good enough.

Perfectionism doesn't fuel motivation; it drains it. It replaces curiosity with anxiety and replaces learning with performance. A young person striving to be perfect isn't chasing excellence — they're running from mistakes. The challenge for parents, teachers, and mentors is to help them shift from a perfection mindset to a *growth mindset*: one that sees mistakes not as proof of inadequacy, but as stepping stones toward mastery.

The Trap of Perfectionism

Perfectionism usually starts with good intentions. A child discovers that success brings praise and attention — the warm glow of approval. Over time, that approval becomes addictive.

"If I do everything right, I'll be loved. If I fail, I'll disappoint."
The brain links achievement to safety.

The result is chronic pressure. The perfectionist brain constantly scans for errors and threats. It avoids challenge because failure feels dangerous. It procrastinates, not out of laziness, but out of fear. And when perfection inevitably fails — because no one can win every time — shame rushes in to fill the gap.

Perfectionism doesn't build resilience; it erodes it. The young person stops asking, *"What can I learn?"* and starts asking, *"What will people think?"* Motivation shifts from exploration to self-protection.

The Growth Mindset Shift

A growth mindset, as psychologist Carol Dweck describes, is the belief that abilities can be developed through effort, strategy, and feedback. It separates identity from performance. You're not good or bad at something — you're *in progress*.

For adolescents, this shift is transformative. When they realize that intelligence and talent aren't fixed traits, failure loses its sting. Struggle becomes data, not defeat. Each mistake is a neural workout that strengthens future performance.

Teaching this mindset doesn't mean pretending that effort alone guarantees success. It means showing that progress and learning depend on persistence, not perfection.

Language Matters

The words adults use can either reinforce perfectionism or nurture growth.

When we say, "You're so smart," we reinforce the idea that ability is innate. When we say, "You worked hard and found a new way," we reinforce effort and strategy. The first breeds pressure; the second builds resilience.

Feedback should highlight *process* — how the student approached a challenge — rather than *personality*. Phrases like:

⇒ "You kept going even when it was tough."

⇒ "I like how you tried a different method."

⇒ "You're learning how to think through problems."

These small shifts reshape how the brain associates effort with reward.

Modeling Imperfection

Young people absorb what adults *do* more than what they *say*. If we model constant stress, self-criticism, or fear of mistakes, they will copy it. But when we model vulnerability — admitting our own errors, laughing at small failures, and showing how we recover — they learn that imperfection is normal and survivable.

Try sharing real stories of setbacks. "I once failed an exam and learned how to study differently," or "I made a mistake at work, but fixing it taught me something valuable." These examples teach self-compassion through honesty.

Redefining Success

Perfectionists measure success by outcomes — the grade, the trophy, the applause. To break that pattern, we need to redefine success as *growth*. Ask young people reflective questions:

- "What did you learn about yourself?"

- "What part of this was hardest, and how did you handle it?"

- "What do you want to try differently next time?"

Each reflection reframes progress as the real prize. When success becomes about learning, the brain's motivation systems stay active even in failure. The dopamine response comes from curiosity, not comparison.

The Fear of Failure

Fear of failure often hides beneath perfectionism. Adolescents worry about disappointing parents, teachers, or themselves. The antidote isn't empty reassurance ("Don't worry, you're great") but unconditional acceptance: "You are loved whether you succeed or not."

When young people believe that failure doesn't threaten belonging, they take healthier risks. They sign up for the competition, try the harder course, apply for the internship — not because they're certain of success, but because they're no longer terrified of falling short.

Failure then transforms into feedback. It becomes part of the story, not the end of it.

Creating Environments That Support Growth

To nurture a growth mindset, the culture around young people must normalize effort and imperfection. In classrooms, celebrate improvement, not just high scores. At home, talk openly about learning curves. Encourage reflection after both success and failure.

Practical strategies include:

1. Celebrate progress. Keep visible reminders of how far they've come — past essays, art, or achievements.

2. De-stigmatize mistakes. Discuss what went wrong and what could be learned.

3. Encourage process goals. Focus on daily habits, not just final outcomes.

4. Model self-compassion. Show that making errors doesn't reduce your worth.

These simple practices shift the emotional climate from fear to freedom.

The Takeaway

Perfectionism is a prison built from good intentions — a desire to be worthy that ends up suffocating growth. The way out is through self-compassion and curiosity.

When young people learn to see mistakes as messages instead of verdicts, they stop defending their image and start developing their potential. They discover that excellence doesn't come from avoiding errors but from learning boldly through them.

Growth mindset isn't just a theory — it's a way of seeing the self. And once that lens changes, perfection loses its power. What remains is something far more enduring: the quiet, confident belief that progress — not perfection — is what truly defines success.

Chapter 17 — Emotions, Energy, and Motivation

How Feelings Fuel (or Drain) Performance

When a teenager says, "I'm just not in the mood," they're not being lazy — they're being honest. Emotion is the invisible engine behind every choice, every effort, every success or failure. We often talk about motivation as if it were purely mental — a matter of logic and discipline — but science tells a different story. Motivation lives in the body as much as in the mind.

Emotion and motivation share the same root: *to move*. Our feelings are signals that tell the brain what's worth pursuing, what to avoid, and how much energy to invest. Understanding this emotional architecture is key to helping young people manage their energy, sustain focus, and recover from burnout.

The Biology of Emotion and Drive

The brain's emotional and motivational systems are deeply intertwined. The limbic system, which processes feelings like joy, fear, and anger, connects directly to the dopamine network, which drives motivation and reward. When an experience triggers positive emotion — excitement, curiosity, pride — the brain releases dopamine and norepinephrine, energizing attention and memory.

But when emotions like fear, shame, or boredom dominate, stress hormones flood the system. The body goes into protection mode, narrowing focus and draining enthusiasm. The adolescent brain, still developing its regulatory circuits, feels these swings more intensely than the adult brain. That's why emotions can make or break motivation in an instant.

Motivation, in essence, is emotional chemistry in motion.

The Myth of "Emotional Control"

Adults often tell young people to "control your emotions," but what we really need to teach is *emotional regulation*. Control implies suppression; regulation means awareness and redirection. Emotions aren't problems to eliminate — they're information to interpret.

When a student feels anxious before a presentation, the emotion isn't the enemy; it's a signal that they care. The goal isn't to erase the feeling, but to transform it into focus. Breathing, reframing thoughts, or preparing more thoroughly can turn anxiety into alertness.

Helping teens name emotions — "I'm nervous," "I'm frustrated," "I'm proud of this" — activates the prefrontal cortex, reducing intensity and improving clarity. Language gives distance; distance gives choice. Once emotion is labeled, it can be leveraged.

Emotional Energy and Motivation Cycles

Every young person has emotional rhythms — natural rises and dips in energy throughout the day or week. Motivation isn't constant, and that's normal. Trying to sustain high intensity 24/7 leads to exhaustion, not excellence.

Teach young people to track their energy patterns. When do they feel most alert? When do they crash? Encouraging self-awareness helps them schedule demanding tasks when their emotional and physical energy peaks.

Recovery is just as vital. Activities that restore energy — music, exercise, rest, time with friends — aren't distractions; they're fuel. The brain needs downtime to reset its reward system. Without it, motivation burns out, leaving apathy in its place.

The Emotional Cost of Pressure

Chronic pressure — from school, sports, or social comparison — floods the body with cortisol. Over time, this stress hormone dulls the dopamine response, making once-exciting goals feel empty. The young person who once loved learning or competition begins to feel numb, detached, or cynical.

Adults can prevent this by creating *psychological safety*: spaces where effort is valued more than outcome and where mistakes don't threaten belonging. Safety restores curiosity, and curiosity restores energy.

When young people feel emotionally safe, their nervous systems shift from survival to exploration. That's where real motivation lives.

Using Emotion as Fuel

Emotions can power action if channeled wisely. Anger can become determination. Fear can become focus. Excitement can become persistence. The key is transformation, not suppression.

Practical steps for teaching emotional fuel:

1. Pause and notice. When emotion spikes, ask, "What am I feeling right now?"

2. Find the message. "What is this emotion trying to tell me?"

3.   Redirect energy. "How can I use this feeling to help me act?"

For example, a frustrated student might say, "I'm angry I didn't do well on this test." The next step: "That means I care. I'll review what went wrong and try again." The emotion stays, but its direction changes.

Adults can reinforce this process through calm curiosity: "What part frustrated you most?" or "What could you do with that energy right now?" This turns emotional storms into learning moments.

Emotional Contagion and Relationships

Motivation doesn't exist in isolation. The emotions of parents, teachers, and peers are contagious. When adults display calm confidence, young people's nervous systems mirror that state. When adults radiate anxiety or frustration, stress spreads instantly.

That's why tone often matters more than words. "You can do this" said with warmth energizes; the same phrase said in irritation depletes. Emotional energy transfers through empathy — a biological phenomenon known as *co-regulation*.

By managing our own emotional state, we help stabilize theirs. Emotional balance is something we give as much as something we teach.

Teaching Emotional Literacy

Building motivation means teaching emotional literacy — the ability to recognize, express, and use feelings constructively. Encourage young people to map emotions along two axes: energy (high to low) and pleasantness (positive to negative).

High energy + pleasant feelings (excitement, enthusiasm) boost motivation.
Low energy + unpleasant feelings (boredom, sadness) lower it.

The goal isn't to stay in one quadrant but to learn how to move through them intentionally. With practice, they'll learn that no emotional state is final — it can be shifted through awareness, action, and rest.

The Takeaway

Motivation isn't just about mindset — it's about emotion in motion. Feelings are not distractions from learning or success; they *drive* them. When young people understand their emotions, they gain control over their energy, focus, and direction.

Adults who help them feel safe, seen, and supported don't just calm their storms — they teach them how to sail. And when young people learn to ride the waves of their own emotions instead of fighting them, they discover the most powerful truth of all: that emotion, once understood, isn't an obstacle to motivation — it's its greatest source.

Chapter 18 — The Role of Rest

How Sleep, Downtime, and Boredom Boost Motivation

In a world that celebrates busyness, rest can look like weakness. Teens wear exhaustion as a badge of honor — late-night studying, endless scrolling, perpetual activity. Adults aren't much better, often modeling the same restless grind. But the truth is simple and biological: the brain cannot stay motivated without rest.

Rest is not the opposite of effort; it's part of it. It's the pause that allows growth, learning, and creativity to consolidate. Sleep, quiet, and even boredom are not distractions from motivation — they are the soil that sustains it. Without recovery, the mind stops generating curiosity, focus, and resilience.

Why the Brain Needs Sleep

Sleep is the most essential — and most ignored — ingredient of motivation. During deep sleep, the brain clears waste, resets stress hormones, and strengthens the neural pathways formed during the day. Memories are filed, connections are reinforced, and emotional balance is restored.

Adolescents, however, are chronically sleep-deprived. Biological shifts in the teenage circadian rhythm push natural sleep onset later, while early school schedules force early waking. The result is an entire generation running on mental fumes.

Studies show that even a single night of poor sleep reduces attention, emotional control, and reward sensitivity — the very systems that drive motivation. Without sleep, effort feels heavier, feedback feels harsher, and goals feel further away.

Encouraging consistent sleep is not about discipline — it's about physiology. Helping teens prioritize rest is like charging the battery that powers every other skill.

Downtime as Brain Training

Rest isn't only about sleep. Quiet, unfocused time is when the brain's default mode network activates — the system that handles reflection, imagination, and meaning-making. When young people stop filling every minute with stimulation, their brains start connecting dots.

That's why insights often come in the shower, on a walk, or before bed. Downtime allows subconscious problem-solving. It's when creativity thrives.

Encourage moments of stillness throughout the day — walking without headphones, journaling, or just lying in silence. These are not "wasted" moments; they are the incubation period for new ideas and deeper understanding.

The Gift of Boredom

Modern life treats boredom like a problem to be solved instantly. But boredom is the brain's signal that it's time to explore, create, or rest. It's a doorway, not a dead end.

When young people learn to tolerate boredom, they rediscover intrinsic motivation — the desire to act from within rather than from external stimulation. Many great ideas begin in the empty spaces between distractions.

Encouraging boredom doesn't mean withholding fun; it means resisting the urge to fill every gap. Let them wander, doodle, daydream. When the mind isn't occupied by constant input, curiosity reawakens on its own.

Rest and Emotional Regulation

Rest isn't just physical — it's emotional. Emotional fatigue is one of the biggest drains on motivation. When teens are constantly managing pressure, social dynamics, and digital overload, their nervous systems stay in survival mode.

Quiet environments, mindful breathing, or simply being in nature allow the nervous system to reset. Heart rate slows, cortisol levels drop, and perspective widens. The brain moves from defense to discovery — the mental shift required for sustained motivation.

Adults can help by modeling emotional rest: setting boundaries, taking breaks, and admitting when they're tired. When young people see rest treated as a responsibility rather than a reward, they learn that recovery is part of strength.

The Rest–Motivation Paradox

The harder we push without recovery, the less productive we become. The prefrontal cortex — the brain's center for planning and focus — tires like a muscle. After prolonged exertion, attention wanes, mistakes rise, and satisfaction falls.

Taking breaks doesn't interrupt motivation; it preserves it. Even short pauses — stretching, hydrating, a few minutes of breathing — restore mental clarity. The brain functions best in cycles: focus, fatigue, rest, renewal.

Encouraging students or children to take restorative breaks during study or creative work isn't indulgence — it's neuroscience in action. The most successful learners are those who know when to rest and when to rise.

Creating a Culture That Values Rest

In many schools and families, rest is earned — a reward for productivity. But when rest becomes conditional, burnout becomes inevitable. Instead, rest should be built into the rhythm of life.

1. Normalize sleep. Talk openly about bedtime routines, digital cutoffs, and the value of feeling rested.

2. Protect downtime. Create "no-plan zones" — evenings or weekends without structured activities.

3. Model balance. Let teens see adults rest without guilt. A parent reading quietly or taking a nap teaches more than any lecture about self-care.

4. Celebrate recovery. Praise the wisdom of pacing oneself: "I like how you took a break and came back stronger."

These practices teach that rest is not laziness — it's literacy in how the body and mind truly function.

The Takeaway

Motivation without rest is like fire without fuel — bright for a moment, then gone. Young people need to know that recovery is not quitting; it's preparation.

Sleep sharpens memory. Downtime restores clarity. Boredom reawakens creativity. Together, they rebuild the energy that makes effort possible.

When we give the brain time to breathe, it rewards us with renewed focus, deeper insight, and lasting motivation. In teaching rest, we teach sustainability — the wisdom of working with, not against, our own biology.

And that lesson might be the most powerful one of all.

Part IV

Purpose, Potential, and Real-World Application

Chapter 19 — Motivation and Mental Health

When Drive Disappears (and How to Bring It Back)

There's a quiet fear many adults carry: "What if my child has lost their spark?" You see it in the student who once cared deeply but now shrugs at everything, or in the young adult who can't find the energy to start what they once loved. When motivation disappears, it can look like laziness or apathy — but often, it's something deeper.

Motivation and mental health are inseparable. The same neural systems that fuel curiosity and effort are also responsible for mood and emotion. When mental health suffers, the brain's reward circuits slow down. Activities that once felt meaningful no longer bring pleasure, and effort feels impossible. Understanding this connection — and responding with compassion rather than frustration — is essential to helping young people recover their drive.

When Motivation Turns Off

At the biological level, motivation depends on *dopamine* — the neurotransmitter that drives anticipation and reward.

Depression, anxiety, chronic stress, and trauma all reduce dopamine activity, making it harder to feel joy or excitement. The result isn't just sadness; it's disconnection. The young person knows what they "should" do but can't feel the internal push to do it.

This isn't defiance — it's depletion. Their brain is signaling, "I'm overloaded." When we meet that exhaustion with pressure ("You just need to try harder"), the gap widens. What they need first is understanding and rest, not urgency.

Motivation doesn't vanish because they don't care; it vanishes because the brain is protecting itself.

The Hidden Faces of Low Motivation

Loss of motivation doesn't always look like depression in the classic sense. It can appear as irritability, withdrawal, distraction, or even perfectionism. A student might overwork to numb anxiety, or underwork to avoid failure. Both patterns stem from emotional overload.

Signs that a young person's low motivation may have mental health roots include:

⇒ Persistent fatigue, even after rest.

⇒ Loss of interest in previously enjoyable activities.

⇒ Changes in sleep or appetite.

⇒ Increased self-criticism or hopelessness.

⇒ Avoidance of social interaction or responsibility.

These aren't personality flaws — they're warning lights. The right response isn't scolding, but curiosity and care.

The Power of Connection

The first step toward restoring motivation is *reconnection*. When someone feels seen, their nervous system begins to stabilize. Safety comes before strategy. Before talking about goals, deadlines, or improvement, ask, "How are you really doing?" and mean it.

Neuroscience shows that social support releases oxytocin and serotonin — chemicals that counteract stress and reawaken the reward system. Simply feeling understood can reignite a small spark of hope.

For adults supporting a struggling teen or young adult, presence matters more than solutions. Sit with them in silence if needed. Offer empathy without rushing to fix. That calm consistency says, "You're not broken, and you're not alone." Motivation grows in the soil of belonging.

Movement and Small Wins

Once emotional safety is restored, the next step is gentle activation. The depressed brain craves movement — not grand plans, but small steps that create momentum. Exercise, sunlight, and creative expression all stimulate dopamine and endorphins, reawakening the motivational network.

The goal isn't productivity; it's *re-engagement with life.* Start small: a ten-minute walk, a short journaling session, a simple task completed. Every small success reminds the brain that action can lead to reward again.

Adults can model and scaffold this process: "Let's do this together," or "How about one small goal for today?" Each tiny victory rebuilds self-trust — the foundation of drive.

Reducing the Pressure to "Bounce Back"

In a culture obsessed with achievement, recovery can feel like failure. Many young people hide their struggles because they fear disappointing others. But mental health doesn't heal under pressure; it heals under patience.

Replace "Why aren't you trying harder?" with "I know this is hard — what would make it a little easier today?" Instead of measuring productivity, focus on stability and self-care.

Motivation will return naturally once the brain no longer feels threatened.

The paradox is that pushing too hard to "get better" often delays improvement. Compassion accelerates recovery because it reduces stress — and stress is the main enemy of motivation.

Professional Help and Hope

Sometimes the loss of motivation signals something more serious — depression, anxiety disorders, burnout, or trauma. In those cases, therapy or counseling is not a sign of weakness but an act of courage. Mental health professionals can help regulate the underlying emotional systems that self-help alone cannot reach.

When young people begin to understand how their brains and emotions interact, shame fades. They realize that their struggle isn't a flaw in character but a symptom of imbalance — one that can be healed.

Recovery doesn't mean returning to who they were before; it means growing into a new version of themselves, wiser and stronger.

The Takeaway

When motivation disappears, look beneath the surface. What seems like indifference may actually be pain, exhaustion, or fear. The remedy isn't discipline but empathy; not punishment but patience.

Mental health is the foundation of motivation. A mind that feels safe, rested, and connected naturally begins to seek meaning and challenge again. Once hope returns — even in the smallest dose — the drive to live, learn, and grow follows.

In helping young people through their lowest moments, we teach them something deeper than persistence. We show them that motivation isn't a constant state — it's a cycle. And even when the spark goes out, it can always, always be rekindled.

Chapter 20 — The Mentor Effect

How One Supportive Adult Can Change a Young Person's Life

Every great story of transformation includes someone who believed before the hero did — a coach, teacher, neighbor, or relative who saw potential beneath the uncertainty. For many young people, that person is the difference between drifting and discovering direction. The science now confirms what experience has long shown: one caring adult can change a life.

The Power of a Singlex Connection

Adolescence is the bridge between dependence and independence, and it can feel unstable. During this time, the brain is remodeling itself — seeking guidance, belonging, and identity. A mentor provides a stabilizing force: a relationship that communicates, *You matter, you're capable, and you're not alone.*

Research on resilience consistently finds that one supportive relationship is the strongest predictor of positive outcomes for youth facing challenges. Psychologist Emmy Werner, in her landmark study on resilience, found that nearly every child who thrived despite hardship had at least one adult who provided emotional security and encouragement. It didn't take many — just one.

Mentorship protects motivation because it restores safety. When young people feel believed in, their stress levels drop, their curiosity returns, and they begin to see themselves through the mentor's eyes: capable and valuable.

Why Mentorship Works

The adolescent brain is wired to learn through modeling. Mentors act as living examples of how to navigate adulthood — how to handle mistakes, pursue goals, and balance emotion with logic. Through empathy and authenticity, they offer something more powerful than advice: *example*.

When a teen observes an adult who listens without judgment, follows through on promises, and treats them as an equal in growth, mirror neurons in the brain activate. These neural systems copy behaviors, tone, and emotional regulation patterns. In essence, a mentor lends their nervous system — modeling calm, curiosity, and persistence until the young person can internalize them.

Mentorship Is Not Perfection

Many adults hesitate to step into a mentoring role because they fear not being "wise enough" or "together enough." But young people don't need flawless mentors — they need *real* ones. Authenticity builds trust far faster than authority. Admitting, "I've made mistakes too," or "I don't have all the answers, but I'll help you figure it out," communicates respect and partnership.

Mentorship is less about giving solutions and more about holding space for discovery. The mentor's role is to listen deeply, ask guiding questions, and reflect back strengths the young person can't yet see.

Emotional Safety First

Trust is the soil in which mentorship grows. Before a mentor can influence behavior or ambition, they must create psychological safety. That means reliability — showing up when promised, keeping confidences, and responding with empathy, not reaction.

Once safety is established, young people begin to open up about their fears and dreams. This vulnerability is sacred territory; how an adult responds in those moments can shape self-esteem for years. The right words — "That makes sense," "You handled that better than you think," "I'm proud of how you tried" — can become internal mantras that carry a young person through future challenges.

The Mentor as Mirror

A great mentor reflects possibility. They don't impose identity; they reveal it. They help the young person see who they're becoming by noticing patterns of strength and potential.

"You're really patient when you teach others."

"You seem happiest when you're creating things."

"You have a natural sense of fairness."

Simple observations like these act as identity cues, helping the young brain link behavior to self-concept. Over time, these reflections form a foundation of confidence and purpose.

Different Forms of Mentorship

Mentors come in many forms:

⇒ Teachers who treat students as thinkers, not just learners.

⇒ Coaches who care about character as much as skill.

⇒ Employers who guide without exploiting.

⇒ Family friends or relatives who provide perspective outside parental roles.

What matters isn't the title but the trust. Formal programs help, but informal moments — a shared meal, a late-night talk, a handwritten note — often leave the deepest mark.

The Ripple Effect

Mentorship doesn't just benefit the mentee. Adults who mentor often experience renewed purpose and optimism. Studies show that mentoring boosts empathy, patience, and even longevity. It reminds adults that their experiences — even their failures — have meaning when shared in service of someone else's growth.

And the ripple doesn't stop there. Young people who are mentored are more likely to become mentors themselves, creating intergenerational chains of care. Motivation multiplies through connection.

How to Be a Transformative Mentor

1. Show up consistently. Reliability communicates worth.

2. Listen more than you speak. Advice matters less than attention.

3.   Notice progress. Point out growth they can't yet see.

4.   Ask reflective questions. "What did that experience teach you?" invites ownership.

5.   Stay curious. Curiosity builds equality — it says, "We're learning together."

The most powerful phrase a mentor can offer isn't "Here's what to do," but "I believe you can figure this out."

The Takeaway

Young people don't need a crowd of admirers — they need one steady believer. One person who notices effort when others overlook it, who listens when others lecture, who stays when things get messy.

The mentor effect isn't magic; it's presence. It's what happens when belief meets consistency. And for a young person navigating uncertainty, that single relationship can ignite the kind of motivation that lasts a lifetime.

Chapter 21 — Coaching Motivation

Practical Strategies for Teachers, Parents, and Leaders

Motivation isn't something we can give to young people like a gift. It's something we help them discover within themselves. The most effective parents, teachers, and leaders aren't commanders; they're coaches — guides who know how to unlock potential through curiosity, structure, and belief.

Coaching motivation doesn't mean pushing harder. It means creating the right mix of challenge and support so that young people learn to push *themselves*. It's about asking better questions, giving meaningful feedback, and building habits that make effort feel rewarding.

The Coaching Mindset

The best motivators think like coaches, not critics. A coach doesn't say, "You failed — you're not good enough." They say, "Let's review what happened and find your next move." The difference is mindset. Critics judge; coaches guide.

To coach effectively, adults must hold two truths at once:

1. You're capable of more than you think.

2. You don't have to be perfect to grow.

When a young person feels both challenged and supported, their motivation system — particularly the prefrontal cortex and dopamine pathways — lights up. The brain loves achievable stretch goals paired with encouragement.

From Commands to Questions

Most adults default to telling: "Do your homework." "Clean your room." "Try harder." But the developing brain responds better to *questions* than commands. Questions activate self-reflection, autonomy, and ownership.

Try these instead:

⇒ "What's your plan for finishing this?"

⇒ "What do you think would make this easier?"

⇒ "What part of this matters to you most?"

Each question invites thinking rather than compliance. When young people articulate their own reasoning, motivation becomes internal — it belongs to them, not to us.

Feedback That Builds Drive

Coaching means guiding performance without crushing confidence. The most powerful feedback combines honesty and empathy. It focuses on behavior, not character:

⇒ "You rushed the last part, and I know you can do it with more focus," instead of "You're careless."

⇒ "I see where you struggled; let's figure out what skill will help next time," instead of "You need to work harder."

This form of feedback triggers the brain's problem-solving mode instead of its defense mechanisms. It tells the young person, "You're still in the game."

Consistency matters even more than brilliance. One encouraging comment, delivered at the right moment, can reset motivation for weeks.

Balancing Challenge and Support

Every effective coach knows the importance of the "optimal challenge zone." Too easy, and students get bored; too hard, and they shut down. The sweet spot is where effort feels meaningful but manageable.

This balance is dynamic. For a confident student, it may mean increasing difficulty. For one who's struggling, it may mean breaking the task into smaller steps. The goal is to keep them in the zone where failure is informative, not defeating.

Support doesn't mean rescuing. It means walking alongside — offering structure without smothering. "I'm here if you need me" is far more powerful than "Let me do it for you."

Building Accountability Without Pressure

Accountability doesn't have to mean punishment. True accountability grows from trust. When young people make commitments in their own words — "I'll finish this by Thursday" — and are gently held to them, motivation strengthens.

Follow up with curiosity, not accusation: "How did that go?" or "What got in the way?" This approach teaches self-reflection and responsibility without shame. Over time, they internalize accountability as self-discipline, not external control.

The Power of Recognition

Recognition fuels motivation — but only when it's specific, authentic, and tied to values. Generic praise fades; meaningful acknowledgment   sticks.
Say, "I noticed you didn't give up when that got frustrating," or "You handled that feedback with maturity." These statements connect achievement to identity and effort, helping the brain associate persistence with pride.

Public recognition can also build community. Highlighting teamwork or kindness reinforces social motivation — the sense that effort matters not only to oneself but to others.

Teaching Reflection

Reflection is the coaching tool that turns experience into growth. After any success or setback, ask three questions:

1. What worked?

2. What didn't?

3. What will you try next time?

Reflection builds metacognition — awareness of one's own learning and motivation patterns. Over time, young people start coaching *themselves*, which is the ultimate goal.

Journals, voice notes, or quick check-ins can make reflection part of routine rather than an afterthought.

Modeling Motivation

Coaching begins with example. Adults who live their own principles — who show curiosity, admit mistakes, and persist through challenge — teach motivation more powerfully than any speech ever could.

When a teacher shares, "I almost gave up on a project too, but I found a new approach," or a parent says, "I'm learning how to be more patient," it normalizes growth. The message becomes, "We're all still learning."

The Takeaway

Motivation can't be forced, but it can be coached. The best coaches listen deeply, challenge wisely, and believe fiercely. They replace pressure with partnership and turn frustration into feedback.

When adults step into that role — calm, curious, consistent — young people begin to internalize their own drive. They stop asking, "Do I have to?" and start saying, "I can do this."

And that moment, quiet and self-chosen, is the birth of real motivation — the kind that lasts long after the coach steps aside.

Chapter 22 — The Language of Motivation

How Words Shape Belief and Behavior

Words are not just sounds — they are signals that shape how the brain interprets the world. For young people, language becomes the architecture of self-belief. Every sentence they hear about who they are, what they can do, and how they should feel builds a story in their mind. Over time, that story becomes their inner voice.

The science of motivation and language reveals a simple truth: what we say — and how we say it — can either light a fire or quietly extinguish it. The words adults use daily can create confidence or cultivate doubt, promote curiosity or fuel defensiveness. Motivation begins with meaning, and meaning begins with language.

Words as Neurochemical Messages

When someone hears encouragement, the brain releases dopamine and oxytocin, chemicals that enhance focus, connection, and willingness to take risks. A calm tone and empathetic phrasing tell the nervous system, "You're safe to try."

In contrast, criticism or sarcasm activates the amygdala, triggering a threat response. The brain shifts from learning mode to self-protection. Even subtle tones — a sigh, an eye roll — can shut down motivation faster than any punishment.

Language literally sculpts the motivational brain. Words don't just describe reality; they create it.

Motivation Begins in How We Speak

The difference between motivating and discouraging language often lies in small shifts:

Discouraging	Motivating
"Why can't you ever focus?"	"What's making it hard to focus right now?"
"You're not trying hard enough."	"Let's figure out what might help you try differently."
"That's wrong."	"That's a good start — let's adjust this part."
"You always mess this up."	"You're still learning this, and that's okay."

Motivating language invites problem-solving instead of shame. It keeps the door to effort open. When young people feel guided instead of judged, they stay engaged long enough to improve.

The Inner Voice We Create

Children and adolescents internalize the language spoken to them. A parent's or teacher's repeated phrase becomes their inner monologue years later:

> ⇒ "You're capable of figuring this out." → builds self-trust.
>
> ⇒ "You never do anything right." → builds self-doubt.

The voice we use with them eventually becomes the one they use with themselves. This is why tone matters as much as content. Encouragement delivered with impatience can still sound like criticism to a sensitive brain.

When adults model self-compassion aloud — "I made a mistake, but I can fix it" — young people learn to speak kindly to themselves. That inner dialogue becomes a renewable source of motivation, especially when external praise fades.

The Power of Naming

Language doesn't just influence emotion — it regulates it. When young people name what they feel ("I'm anxious," "I'm excited," "I'm frustrated"), the prefrontal cortex activates and the limbic system calms down. This process, called **affect labeling**, helps transform chaos into clarity.

Encourage emotional vocabulary. Replace "I feel bad" with "I feel disappointed" or "I feel tense." The more precisely emotions are named, the more control the brain gains. Emotional literacy is motivational literacy — it allows young people to manage the feelings that block effort.

Encouraging Through Framing

How adults frame challenges changes how young people experience them. Saying "You *have to* finish this" signals pressure; saying "You *get to* practice this skill" signals opportunity.

Reframing effort as exploration — "Let's see how far you can go with this," "What can you learn from this mistake?" — transforms struggle into curiosity. This language shift activates the brain's reward pathways, linking growth with pleasure rather than fear.

Even failure can be reframed:

⇒ "You failed" → "You discovered what doesn't work."

⇒   "You're behind" → "You're still building the foundation."

Each phrase tells a different story about who they are and what's possible next.

Listening as Language

Motivating language isn't only about speaking — it's about listening. When young people feel heard, their defenses drop, and their willingness to engage increases. Listening validates identity. It says, "Your voice matters here."

Active listening means paraphrasing feelings — "It sounds like you're frustrated because you worked hard" — and asking clarifying questions instead of rushing to advise. Listening creates space where motivation can take root naturally.

In that silence, young people often find their own solutions. The most powerful motivational language sometimes contains no words at all.

Language That Builds Identity

Every time we describe a young person, we influence how they see themselves. Calling someone "lazy" or "shy" locks them into a fixed identity. Instead, describe behaviors as temporary:

"You're acting tired today," or "You seemed quiet this week." This distinction tells the brain, *You can change.*

Likewise, identity-based affirmations like "You're the kind of person who keeps trying" strengthen motivation through self-consistency. Once someone sees persistence as part of who they are, their brain works harder to maintain that identity.

The Takeaway

Motivation lives in language. The words we choose shape how young people think, feel, and act. A well-timed phrase can lower anxiety, rekindle confidence, or reframe a failure as progress.

When we replace judgment with curiosity, commands with questions, and labels with descriptions, we create communication that builds rather than breaks. Over time, our words become their beliefs — and those beliefs determine how far they'll go.

In the end, motivation isn't built on lectures or slogans. It's built in conversation — one kind word, one curious question, one moment of genuine listening at a time.

Chapter 23 — The Culture of Motivation

Building Communities Where Young People Thrive

Motivation doesn't develop in isolation. It's shaped, sustained, and sometimes silenced by the culture around us — the unspoken messages about what matters, what's possible, and who belongs. For young people, that culture includes families, schools, teams, online spaces, and friend groups. Each of these environments either nourishes or drains their natural drive to grow.

When we talk about "motivating" the next generation, we often focus on individuals: how to change habits, build grit, or improve focus. But personal strategies can only go so far if the broader culture rewards perfectionism, competition, or fear. To help young people thrive, we must create cultures that make motivation the norm — not through pressure, but through purpose, connection, and care.

What Culture Teaches the Brain

Every community teaches implicit lessons. A classroom where mistakes are punished teaches caution. A family that values curiosity over correctness teaches courage. The adolescent brain, especially between ages 10 and 25, is a social sponge. It learns what to care about by watching what others care about.

Culture literally rewires the brain's reward system. When effort, kindness, or learning are celebrated, those behaviors release dopamine and feel good. When only outcomes or appearances are rewarded, motivation becomes fragile — dependent on external validation.

The key question for any group that serves young people is simple: *What do we reward here?*

Belonging as the Foundation

A culture of motivation begins with belonging. Humans are tribal creatures, and adolescents even more so. If they feel excluded, unsafe, or unseen, their brains divert energy from learning to protection. Only when belonging is secure can motivation return.

Belonging doesn't mean agreement; it means acceptance. Young people need to know they can show up as themselves — with their quirks, emotions, and questions — without fear of ridicule. When they do, effort becomes an act of expression rather than survival.

Communities that value belonging build psychological safety through kindness, humor, and inclusion. The message is simple but transformative: *You matter here.*

Shared Purpose Over Competition

Many modern environments, especially schools and sports, are built on comparison. Competition can inspire excellence — but when overemphasized, it breeds anxiety, jealousy, and burnout. In competitive cultures, young people often work to *avoid losing* rather than to *discover meaning.*

The most motivating communities replace rivalry with shared purpose. A classroom that frames learning as teamwork ("We're solving this together") fosters collaboration. A sports team that emphasizes personal growth over winning creates athletes who play for love, not fear.

Shared purpose activates the brain's social reward circuits — cooperation feels good because it strengthens connection. Motivation then becomes collective, not competitive.

The Role of Adults as Cultural Architects

Every adult who interacts with youth is a culture-builder. Teachers set the emotional climate of classrooms; coaches set the tone of effort and resilience; parents establish the home's emotional rhythm.

Adults create culture through small, repeated actions — tone, consistency, and values in motion. Do we celebrate curiosity or only results? Do we model rest as essential or treat it as indulgence? Do we listen before correcting?

Young people internalize these answers more deeply than any lecture. Culture is built not by slogans on the wall, but by the stories told in daily behavior.

Encouraging Collective Growth

A thriving motivational culture values *progress together*. This means celebrating not just individual success, but community improvement — when a class learns to collaborate better, when a team supports a struggling player, when a family navigates conflict with patience.

Practical ways to cultivate collective motivation include:

1.   Shared reflection. Regularly ask, "What went well for us this week? What can we improve together?"

2.   Visible values. Display and discuss principles like respect, courage, curiosity, or kindness — and link them to real actions.

3.   Mutual accountability. Replace punishment with partnership: "We're all responsible for making this space work."

4.   Peer mentorship. Pair older or more experienced members with younger ones to model growth and support.

Communities that grow together sustain motivation naturally, because everyone's progress matters.

Digital Culture and Its Impact

Online environments now shape youth motivation as much as physical ones. Social media creates microcultures where likes and followers become currency. While these platforms can connect and inspire, they can also distort values — rewarding image over substance.

Adults can guide young people to build healthier digital cultures by asking reflective questions:

⇒   "What kind of community do you want to be part of online?"

⇒   "How do you feel after spending time with certain groups or creators?"

⇒ "Are your digital spaces lifting you up or wearing you down?"

When youth learn to curate their digital environments intentionally, they begin to protect their motivation from the noise of constant comparison.

The Ripple Effect

A culture of motivation spreads through example. One teacher who listens deeply can shift the tone of an entire school. One family who prioritizes connection over control can inspire relatives and friends. One team that celebrates effort over victory can redefine success for a community.

Motivational culture is contagious — and it starts small. Every kind word, every moment of patience, every story of growth adds to the collective energy that says, "We learn, we grow, we try again."

The Takeaway

Individual motivation thrives in collective health. When young people live in environments that value curiosity, compassion, and resilience, their drive becomes self-sustaining. They don't work just to achieve; they work to contribute.

The most powerful cultures are those that whisper, through every   interaction: "You belong. Your effort matters. And together, we can do something extraordinary."

That's the kind of culture that doesn't just motivate young people — it shapes the kind of adults they'll become.

Chapter 24 — Parenting for Motivation

Raising Self-Driven, Not Pressure-Driven Kids

Every parent wants their child to be motivated — to study, to practice, to take initiative, to care. But beneath that wish often lies a fear: *What if they never find their drive?* In the rush to push them forward, many parents unintentionally do the opposite — replacing genuine motivation with anxiety, and curiosity with compliance.

True motivation can't be forced from the outside; it grows from the inside. Parenting for motivation isn't about control or constant encouragement — it's about creating conditions where effort feels safe, meaningful, and rewarding. It's less about pushing harder and more about building trust, autonomy, and emotional connection.

The Parent as Motivational Climate

Parents are the first environment a child ever knows. Their tone, expectations, and reactions become the emotional climate in which motivation either flourishes or fades. When children feel loved only when they perform, their brains link achievement with safety. They begin to chase approval rather than curiosity.

In contrast, when parents communicate unconditional acceptance — "I love you no matter what happens today" — the nervous system relaxes. The child's energy can then go toward exploration and effort instead of self-protection.

Motivation needs oxygen, not pressure. Parents provide that oxygen through warmth, consistency, and genuine belief.

From Pressure to Partnership

Pressure often comes disguised as care: "I just want you to do your best." But to a young person, those words can sound like a demand, especially if "best" always seems just out of reach. The brain under pressure releases cortisol, narrowing attention and creativity. Over time, the joy of learning or striving disappears, replaced by fear of letting someone down.

Partnership, by contrast, says: "We're on the same side. Let's figure this out together." It shifts focus from performance to process. Instead of asking, "Did you win?" or "What grade did you get?" try:

⇒   "What did you enjoy about it?"

⇒   "What part was hard, and how did you handle it?"

⇒ "What did you learn about yourself?"

These questions invite reflection and ownership. The child stops performing *for* the parent and starts working *for* themselves.

Autonomy: The Secret Ingredient

Self-driven kids are not the ones who follow every rule perfectly — they're the ones who make thoughtful choices. To reach that point, they need autonomy: the sense that their actions come from their own will.

Neuroscience shows that autonomy activates the brain's reward system more strongly than external control. When children feel trusted to make decisions, dopamine reinforces that ownership, strengthening intrinsic motivation.

Parents can build autonomy by offering structured choices:

⇒ "Would you rather do homework before or after dinner?"

⇒ "Do you want to sign up for soccer or guitar this season?"

Even small choices build the feeling of agency — the belief that "my effort makes a difference."

Modeling Motivation

Children learn far more from watching how parents live than from hearing what they say. When adults pursue goals, show persistence, or admit when they're learning something new, they model motivation in real time.

Share your process openly: "This project is hard for me, but I'm going to keep trying." When kids see adults struggle without giving up, they internalize that resilience.

Likewise, show balance. A parent who never rests teaches exhaustion; a parent who rests with purpose teaches sustainability. Motivation isn't about endless hustle — it's about rhythm.

Praise That Builds, Not Breaks

Well-intentioned praise can backfire. "You're so smart" sounds encouraging, but it ties worth to outcome. When children later struggle, they may conclude, "Maybe I'm not smart anymore."

Instead, praise effort, strategy, and perseverance: "You really stuck with that," "You found a new way to solve it," or "I admire how patient you were." This feedback shifts focus from being good to *getting better*. It reinforces a growth mindset — the belief that abilities develop through effort.

Avoid rescuing when frustration appears. Step in with empathy, not solutions: "I see this is hard — want to take a break and try again together?" Support teaches confidence; rescue teaches helplessness.

Managing Expectations

Parents often carry invisible expectations about success — the right school, career, or path. But children aren't projects; they're people discovering their own meaning.

Motivation fades when it's driven by fear of disappointing others. It thrives when linked to personal values. Ask: "What kind of person do you want to be?" "What matters most to you about this?" These questions help young people anchor drive to identity, not approval.

A child who knows *why* they're doing something will push harder and recover faster than one who's simply told *to* do it.

Repairing When Pressure Has Gone Too Far

Every parent slips into overcontrol sometimes — it comes from love. What matters is repair. When you notice your words have discouraged rather than inspired, be honest: "I think I pushed too hard earlier. I trust you to find your way." That humility rebuilds safety.

Repair teaches children that relationships — like motivation — are flexible and forgiving. It shows them that pressure can give way to partnership, and mistakes can lead to reconnection.

The Takeaway

Parenting for motivation is not about manufacturing drive — it's about protecting it. It means shifting from control to connection, from pressure to partnership, from perfection to presence.

When young people feel seen, supported, and trusted, motivation becomes self-sustaining. They work not to prove their worth, but to express it.

The greatest gift a parent can give is not constant encouragement, but steady belief: "I know you can handle this. I'm here when you need me."

That quiet confidence teaches more about motivation than any lecture ever could

Epilogue — The Hope Equation

Why Generation Z and Alpha Might Be the Most Motivated Yet

It's easy to look at today's world — with its constant noise, its digital distractions, its waves of uncertainty — and worry that young people are losing their drive. Headlines warn of burnout, disengagement, and short attention spans. Teachers lament shrinking curiosity; parents see anxiety where ambition used to be. But behind the worry lies a quieter truth: this generation is not unmotivated — it's redefining motivation itself.

Every era faces its crisis of meaning. The postwar generation sought stability; the baby boomers chased prosperity; millennials pursued balance. Generation Z and Alpha have inherited a world that demands something deeper: purpose. And because of that, they may become the most motivated generations humanity has ever seen — not in the traditional sense of obedience or achievement, but in the modern sense of alignment, where effort follows values, not fear.

The Old Equation Is Breaking

For much of modern history, motivation was built on external scaffolding: rules, rewards, and reputations. Do well in school to get into college. Get a degree to get a job. Work hard to earn respect. Those formulas worked — until they didn't.

Today's young people grew up watching those systems fracture. They've seen adults burned out, overworked, and underfulfilled. They've watched the planet strain, economies wobble, and institutions lose credibility. The promise of "work hard and you'll be fine" no longer feels true. So they're asking better questions: *What's the point? What's worth my energy? What kind of life actually matters?*

This questioning isn't apathy; it's discernment. When traditional motivators collapse, internal ones rise. That shift — from compliance to conscience — may be the greatest motivational leap in centuries.

The New Motivational Landscape

Unlike previous generations, Gen Z and Alpha have grown up with constant information, connection, and choice. These can be overwhelming forces, yes — but they're also unprecedented tools for meaning. The same technologies that fragment attention also democratize passion. A 14-year-old can learn coding on YouTube, start a microbusiness on TikTok, or join global movements for climate justice before finishing high school.

They're not waiting for permission. They're inventing the pathways themselves. This self-directed energy — when guided by emotional literacy and purpose — is the essence of intrinsic motivation.

They also crave authenticity. Traditional motivators like status, titles, or empty praise no longer impress them. They're moved by transparency, empathy, and real-world impact. They want work that matters, mentors who listen, and systems that match their values. This may frustrate adults who equate motivation with obedience, but it signals evolution: drive is no longer about fitting in — it's about *belonging to something real.*

From Achievement to Alignment

The emerging motivational model is less linear and more personal. Success is no longer a race to the top; it's a journey toward coherence — living in alignment with one's principles.

For Generation Z, mental health and motivation are intertwined. They understand that burnout isn't a badge of honor, that rest fuels creativity, and that emotional awareness enhances performance. They are rewriting the rules of productivity from the inside out.

This balance — of ambition with empathy, of speed with sustainability — is something earlier generations often missed.

If nurtured, it could make them not only more driven but also more humane.

Resilience in an Age of Uncertainty

These young generations were shaped by instability: pandemics, political turmoil, climate anxiety, rapid technological change. But rather than breaking them, these experiences have built emotional adaptability — the true core of modern grit.

They are growing up fluent in uncertainty, constantly recalibrating their plans and identities in real time. This flexibility, though stressful, may be their superpower. Motivation in the 21st century will belong not to those who never falter, but to those who can pivot without losing purpose.

The world they're inheriting rewards creativity, collaboration, and courage — all qualities that thrive when fear-based motivation fades.

The Rise of Purpose-Driven Motivation

Psychologists have long known that humans perform best when their goals feel meaningful. Today's youth seem to understand this intuitively. Surveys show that Gen Z ranks purpose and social impact higher than salary in career decisions. They're driven by causes — equality, environment, mental health, justice — that transcend personal gain.

Purpose transforms effort into identity. It turns "I have to" into "I choose to." And when that shift occurs, motivation becomes exponential. You no longer need to push people who believe their work makes a difference — they pull themselves forward.

This collective orientation toward purpose could spark the most globally conscious generation yet — one motivated not by fear of failure, but by the hope of contribution.

The Emotional Revolution

One of the most overlooked reasons for optimism is emotional literacy. Generations Z and Alpha are the first to grow up with open conversations about mental health, empathy, and vulnerability. They know that feelings are not flaws; they're feedback.

This awareness gives them a motivational edge. A person who understands their own emotions can regulate stress, recover from failure, and build resilience. Instead of suppressing fear, they learn from it. Instead of denying sadness, they seek connection.

They are dismantling the old myth that motivation requires emotional toughness. They're replacing it with something more sustainable: *emotional truth*. That truth — the ability to feel fully and act wisely — will be the new fuel of human progress.

The Mentor Generation

Paradoxically, the most self-directed generation still longs for guidance — not authority, but mentorship. They want adults who model curiosity, integrity, and humility. They crave genuine relationships where listening matters more than lecturing.

This creates an extraordinary opportunity. If older generations shift from commanding to coaching, the motivational potential of youth will skyrocket. The combination of digital fluency and emotional support could become the most powerful driver of innovation the world has ever seen.

Every generation has a role in this equation. The young bring energy and vision; adults provide stability and wisdom. When those forces meet in partnership, hope turns into progress.

The Hope Equation

If motivation is energy multiplied by meaning, then hope is its long-term formula. Hope doesn't mean blind optimism; it means belief in the possibility of improvement — the conviction that effort still matters.

For Generation Z and Alpha, hope looks different. It's not naïve or idealistic; it's pragmatic and collective. It's the hope of climate activists who plant trees they may never sit under, the hope of creators who use technology to amplify empathy, the hope of students who speak up for those unheard.

Hope, when joined with action, becomes the purest form of motivation. It's what keeps people learning, connecting, and caring even in dark times. And that, perhaps more than anything, defines this generation: they haven't given up. They're still trying.

The Future of Drive

We often assume that motivation is declining because it doesn't look the same as it once did. But perhaps it's evolving — from obedience to ownership, from performance to purpose, from competition to connection.

The next generation isn't unmotivated; they're unconvinced by empty goals. They want meaning before movement, belonging before achievement. And once they find that alignment, their energy is unstoppable.

The task for parents, teachers, mentors, and leaders is not to reignite their fire — it's to *protect it*. Give them room to rest, to question, to feel, to fail, and to rebuild. Trust that the drive is already there, waiting for a direction worthy of it.

Because motivation is not dying. It's maturing. And if we listen, learn, and lead beside them, Generation Z and Alpha may just remind us of something we've forgotten:

That hope — the belief that effort still matters — is not the opposite of struggle. It's the engine that turns struggle into strength.

And in that equation — Hope × Purpose × Connection = Motivation — lies not only the future of the next generation, but the renewal of our own.